Human Art

Understanding your own personal design

Everyone Is a Masterpiece

Brook & Rod Thornley

Artwork by Donna O. Kearney

BROOK DESIGN COMPANY & HUMAN ART, LLC

ISBN 978-0-9790624-0-7
ISBN 978-0-9790624-1-4   (special edition)

Brook Design Company & Human Art, LLC
www.human-art-design.com

To all mankind…one person at a time.

CONTENTS

Forward

As I walk through a museum of fine art, I enter each room anticipating the beauty I know I'll encounter there. I feel a tingle of excitement. Which piece of art will I love? Which will I appreciate? Will I see some that I won't understand? As I am strolling by each piece, I realize that the great thing about art is that it's a personal experience. People choose the pieces that speak to them on an emotional level. I wonder what piece, in each room I enter, will speak to me. When I find it, I know the lines and color of the piece will communicate what I need emotionally. My response will resonate deep inside me.

For some reason we have forgotten to look at each human being in this same way. People are masterpieces that we come upon or experience in life as if we are entering their space in a museum. They touch us on an emotional level. The lines and colors in their bodies—their unique compositions—communicate to us. Have we forgotten to look at them with the same open eyes that we have when we pass through the doors of an art museum? Do we feel the anticipation of finding that connection deep inside in response to each person's own beauty? Or have we learned in some way to pass by and discount them in a search for that ultimate personification of "beauty"—as if all humans were pieces in an exhibit, but only one truly great piece of art existed? We need to open our eyes to see the art and beauty in every human being. We are each truly unique, a masterpiece. We are all imprints of many frequencies, and we leave that emotional imprint of our beauty wherever we go. No one will ever experience anything just like us again.

When I see someone new, perhaps I'll love and appreciate her beauty. Or maybe I just won't understand it. I am not alone. Most of us don't understand the beauty we find in others. We don't recognize the masterpieces we encounter each day. We lack the information, skills or rules to interpret them. We don't know their "equations." Just as solving math or chemistry problems is impossible without understanding the rules, in art—especially Human Art—we as a society have reached a point of discounting what we can't comprehend merely because we lack the tools and rules to do so.

I love walking through the "exhibit" of life! I relish observing this beautiful world and these intriguing pieces of art—humans—that I encounter daily. Using the "rules," or the science of color and line, I am able to grasp people's beauty in a way that extends far beyond the physical surface. My experience of *your* beauty starts the moment I first get a glimpse of you. Your communication, the lines in your nose, the way you walk, the way you talk, the way you process your information, are all pieces of the equation, and I start summing them up, emotionally. Without fail, each time I say, "Yes, this is the piece for me!" You touch me at that level because, unlike a painting or a piece of pottery, you are alive, and you use your "equation"—your beauty, talents and strengths—to act and interact *with* me. I've yet to find the sculpture that can do that. Understanding the right rules and using the right tools to unlock the mystery of human composition has enabled me to stand back in reverential, open-mouthed awe as I contemplate the greatest beauty of all: *you.*

CHAPTER I

Overview of HUMAN ART THEORY & PRACTICE

TRYING TO CATEGORIZE AND DEFINE DIFFERENT TYPES OF HUMAN BEAUTY HAS BEEN ONE OF HUMANKIND'S FAVORITE PASTIMES. EACH BRANCH OF THIS PARTICULAR KIND OF SCIENCE HAS TOUCHED ON CORRECT PRINCIPLES, BUT MOST HAVE NOT DELVED DEEP ENOUGH INTO THE SUM TOTAL OF WHO WE ARE. THE CONCEPT OF HUMAN ART IS COMPOSED OF DESIGN, ART AND BEHAVIORAL PRINCIPLES THAT ARE ORGANIZED INTO A METHODOLOGY. THE PRINCIPLES ARE EMPIRICAL, MEANING YOU CAN OBSERVE THEM. YOU CAN TRACE THEM CONSISTENTLY THROUGHOUT NATURE, ANIMALS AND MOST IMPORTANTLY, HUMAN BEINGS.

The methodology has been observed over many years. It is consistent. It works. The principles find their way through everything you see around you. Everything in nature has an order, including mankind. We seem to recognize this order at some level, but in the general melee of life, we somehow lose sight of it. Human Art awakens us to who we really are. It is a measurement, an equation that finally makes sense of our divine nature and how we were made. It gives us back something that we came to this wonderful earth with, but of which we somehow lost sight. Human Art is a gift; it doesn't change who we are, it simply helps us recognize ourselves. It points out all the wonderful qualities and traits that we all uniquely possess, and in helping us to get to know ourselves better, it gives us a glimpse of what we can do with our lives. Consequently, it empowers us and gives us a direction for greatness in life that is totally individual.

Human Art is about understanding these principles and striving for harmony in the way we live our lives. Anyone who loves music knows what a thrill flawless harmony can produce. Perfectly chosen notes, ringing together, can inspire a myriad of feelings and be a powerfully emotional experience. Other kinds of harmony are just as affecting. Any pleasing combination of elements seems to speak to us.

In Human Art, perfect harmony can actually be measured through four basic design elements: color, line, movement and sound. These are characteristics that are consistently grouped together when you observe anything harmonious. You'll find that where one exists, either in nature or a human being, so do the others. They cross-reference each other. I believe that we all understand this harmony at a subconscious level. Bringing it to a conscious awareness and understanding will lead to an appreciation of all the beauty around us.

Until now, we have lacked an organized way to truly measure the uniqueness of individuals and define their attractiveness. To argue that color and the elements that go with it can measure a person's uniqueness is to argue your own reaction to a specific color. When exposed to a color, you have an experience. Why else would you have a "favorite" color? I know two sisters who argued vehemently all through early childhood about which color was "better," red or blue. Each little girl was so convinced her favorite color had an innate superiority that the arguments sometimes led to tears, much to their parents' bewilderment. Of course, both girls were right, because they were describing the effect that the color of choice had on *them*.

COLOR, LINE, MOVEMENT & SOUND

Color, line, movement and sound all work together and can be grouped or measured because they are harmonious. Human Art teaches that a particular color and line have a correlating movement as well as a correlating sound. For example, if I wanted to portray something animated, I would use a color with white added to it. White creates an ambiance of youthfulness and fun. I would then use its correlating line, which is a circular line. This line creates a bubbling feel. If I wanted to enhance that scene even more, I would add its harmonious movement, which is buoyant. So, we start with a nice, whitened blue. We then turn it into a bubble, in fact many bubbles. Then we add the quick, buoyant movement of a babbling brook, and finally we can hear the quickness in the sound of the stream babbling. There you have it: animation with its correlating color, line, movement and sound.

Now, visualize an animated person. When she walks into a room, she's the embodiment of a babbling brook. She is invigorating and fun, full of energy and bounce—like a bunny rabbit. She talks a lot and bounces from person to person just as any animated object would.

People already possess their equation, or communication—they do not have to learn it. *We* just have to see it. We look for the lines in their bodies and when we know what the lines mean, we begin calculating. Then we hear these people talk and watch them move. If we're paying attention, we can recognize that all their characteristics correlate, and then we see it: their greatness.

Ignorance would have it that only one type of line is beautiful, and if we don't possess that line, we are simply not attractive. But as ridiculous as that idea is, in a way don't we believe it? When

If I wanted to portray something animated, I would use a color with white added to it.

we study art or design in any form, we recognize how important each and every line is as it harmonizes with color to create a complete effect. But if we see that same line in a person, for some reason we forget to extend to him or her the same courtesy. For example, I envision a fine sculpture that is large, angular and bold. Its beauty is strong and rustic. I imagine it in the family room or den of my home, and I anticipate that visitors in my home will praise the rustic beauty it communicates. Yet, what if that same angular line or communication happens to be, say, someone's nose? Many people would consider such a nose *not* beautiful. Why? The line still conveys the same message of strength and wonder—it is one small clue as to what that person is all about.

In a similar analogy, if we were to do a painting and wanted to communicate grace and elegance, we would use a very flowing line to create that essence. The same principle applies to people. If they have flowing lines in their bodies, then their beauty consists of grace and elegance.

I envision a fine sculpture that
is large, angular and bold.

For an expression of stillness, we would use a straight line. Once again, if a person has this line in her body, she also communicates and moves in that same manner. Everything about her is harmonious, a simple communication of what she is about. That communication is what it all boils down to when we look at people and experience their beauty. It's a message about not only what people look like, but more importantly who they are, where their strengths lie and how they communicate and interact with others.

Understanding that we were not made by chance is helpful in comprehending these ideas. No accident could produce something so wonderful. A higher power carefully and purposefully put us together with our own combination of color, lines, movement and sound. I believe in this kind of creation because of all the thousands of people that have been "measured" through this methodology, not one person's body has told a lie about who he or she is, and yet every single person has been different. We're unique, like snowflakes, and just as breathtaking. Would you spend your time in the winter trying to search through all the different snowflakes in your yard to decide which one was the most beautiful? Or would you be perfectly content to catch one on your mitten and examine it closely, accepting it and marveling at its individual beauty. So, instead of looking for that one communication of greatness, how about looking for greatness one person at a time? Diving in and figuring out one person's distinction is so exciting! Each piece of Human Art is a priceless masterpiece that is nowhere else in existence.

PERSONAL CASES

A few examples of some of the literally thousands of people
I've worked with over the years will illustrate what I am saying.

One of my favorite Human Art stories is about a woman who has been with our company for many years. She really understands Human Art and all that it entails, but when she was younger she felt as though she didn't fit in anywhere. She was not a cheerleader, in the band or in any group in school. She struggled to understand her worth and figure out where she fit in. One day in high school she finally found something that she thought she could do—what she believed at the time was her niche. She had decided to run track. Well, the day came for her to run to record her time. The distance wasn't great, but enough to show the onlookers, her peers, her newfound skill. She and a friend decided to give it their all. When they were signaled to go, the two of them started off, running side by side. Suddenly, they heard a roar of approval from the stands. Their elation was short-lived, however, when to their dismay they realized that the crowd was roaring alright—with laughter. The woman recounted later that when she looked over at her companion she realized that the two of them bore an uncanny resemblance to a pair of chickens running for their lives. Deflated and embarrassed, she vowed never to run in public again and left her high school years, along with her confidence, behind.

Years later, she came to Human Art and was reminded of who she is and where her beauty lies. She learned the way her harmonies lined up and what that communicated to others. To our surprise, she had spent her entire life till then completely unaware of what was obvious to us: her greatness. Watching her learn was like watching her wake up as she discovered that she *did* have a place on this earth—a very important one. She has sophistication and grace, she is a concrete thinker and she possesses true elegance. She is serious and yet fun in a very warm way. She thinks in terms of black and white, and yet is very creative at the same time. She holds a power that no one else does. She finally found that power, and with it, her attractiveness. Most importantly, she found out that she had *always* had both. She had not been able to see, although others certainly could, that she was and is truly beautiful.

$\mathcal{A}$nother example involves a woman we met who was related to the blackened design (which we will soon learn all about). The colors she related to were rustic: pure, chroma color with black mixed in. Her bone structure was very defined. She related to angular lines. Her sound and movement were deliberate and task oriented. You could actually hear her walk through the door, although she wasn't a large woman. Her beauty was natural, rich and exotic.

She claimed to possess no beauty. This was rubbish! We began the process of teaching her the inherent qualities she had, repeating her harmony all throughout her dress, makeup and hair. We then taught her about the innate qualities in her personality and how she acts and interacts with people. After the process was complete, she came back from vacation and described with tears in her eyes what it was like to be singled out in a crowd at a show as being the most beautiful woman in the room. What a contrast to the experiences she had been accustomed to before.

$\mathcal{Y}$et another illustration involves a person who had a very still design. The lines in her body were straight and simple. She stood very tall. She related to pure, chroma color. She had spent a good amount of her life feeling like people were cool to her, when in reality their demeanor was a reaction of respect to her inherent qualities. People responded to her in a similar manner to how we all stand a little taller and become more proper when we walk into a black tie event. She learned quickly, to her shock, that people were sometimes a little intimidated by her, and a simple smile directed towards the awestruck person usually solved the problem.

I could go on and on. I've met so many people who thought they had no beauty, when in fact they just didn't *understand* it. We all have different lines. Our noses, our hands, *every* line in our body communicates clues as to what makes us tick. Too often, people spend too much time trying to change the very lines in their body that communicate some of their most endearing traits. A beautiful painting would never try so desperately to hide all of its elegant and refined lines from the world, just because it isn't, say, the Mona Lisa. We don't want every painting to be the Mona Lisa. A landscape is just as valuable as a still life, which is just as lovely as a portrait. Their different lines are how you recognize what they are. No one has to tell you, "Hey, don't get this mixed up with the Mona Lisa. This one's a lake at sunset." You know when you see it. More importantly, you recognize and feel it.

That instant recognition applies to sound, too. The refined music of an orchestra can give you the same feeling as seeing a scarf blowing in the wind, or a figure skater with long limbs gliding on the ice. That sound and those lines are harmonious. They create the same feeling. Silence is sound, too. The quiet white field of clean snow in the cool, still air can communicate the same feeling as a beautiful, silver, contemporary sculpture.

We all have different amounts of color, line, sound and movement. They communicate our own unique imprint. The empowering part of this concept comes when we stop looking externally for our own greatness and instead find the equation within ourselves. Or, if we are fortunate enough to have in some way found it, we can dig even deeper and discover some things about ourselves that are sleeping. To look at it from another angle, some (unfortunately too few) of us are lucky enough to be very happy with ourselves, but perhaps we don't always understand others as well. When we apply the principles of Human Art, we start celebrating, rather than restricting, what we like about ourselves and others.

Everyone has an inherent frequency pattern—like a harmonic chord, a palate of colors, a signature, or voiceprint. This imprint is carried in the nucleus of every cell and forms our natural tendencies, our body design, and even our personality traits. We could call this pattern our original understructure.

But as we move though life's many challenges, we experience differing levels of human endeavor—such as thinking, acting, feeling, and even creating. Each time we think or act, for instance, we send a secondary wave pattern that overlays our permanent imprint, changing our conscious state or way of seeing, our mode of functioning, or our mood.

Like strings of a guitar that resonate with a certain harmonic quality, our own imprint is distinct. And yet, as we move over these strings in cadences short and sweet, deep and low, or maybe high and quick, our heart follows, changing our mood and physiology along with the melody.

— Carole Coombs

The Benefits of Using Human Art

The benefits of Human Art are many. The most significant one is that finally you will be able to specifically define your own communications and how you were put together. You will comprehend where your greatness lies and how to use and strengthen it to be the best you can be. You will know what it's like to look at you and to be around you, almost from an outside perspective. You will fully embrace your beauty—and that goes for men and women. Men and women are both beautiful—so many different communications of beautiful. Words cannot begin to describe the effect Human Art has had on people. To be able to pinpoint your uniqueness is so empowering, and to see others learn about themselves and then really go with it is so gratifying! The most exciting part is that most of us already have an innate sense of our own design. In my years of helping people truly learn about themselves, I've realized that most of them already, deep down, "knew" it, they just didn't *know* it.

Over the years we have also found Human Art to be helpful, almost critical, to success in several different fields. The following is a short list of just a few areas where the Human Art methodology can be profoundly influential.

- Cosmetology
- Interior Design
- Wardrobe
- Human Resource Management
- Sales
- Team Building
- Leadership

You will comprehend where your greatness lies and how to use and strengthen it to be the best you can be.

Human Art was created out of a firm commitment to the basic premise that every person is an attractive, unique and intrinsically valuable human being. Our intention is to help each customer personally experience this truth through increased awareness of what his or her design communicates and to provide comprehensive design services to enhance inner and outer beauty.

Brook (myself) and Rod (my husband) Thornley established Human Art in Salt Lake City, Utah. I am a licensed cosmetologist with over 25 years of experience in the field of personal design, including hair, makeup and wardrobe design. Rod is a licensed Clinical Social Worker who graduated from the University of Utah. Rod and I have worked together to correlate color principles with art therapy and color theory in psychology. The Human Art program is based on the work and case studies of Johannes Itten, the color theory of Wilhelm Ostwald, studies by Dr. Max Luscher, Faber Birren, Debora Clarke and Donald Weismann, as well as local researchers Carole Coombs, Donna Boam and Donna O. Kearney. Over the years, this unique methodology has changed the lives of hundreds of customers. We have received innumerable letters and personal testimonials asserting that our work has made a genuine impact in the areas of enhanced personal attractiveness and satisfaction, increased sense of self-esteem, improved communication with others, and even expanded business success.

What Is Human Art?

Human Art is a personal design system (a methodology) which measures the individual's unique attributes, physical characteristics and personality style. By combining design, art, color and psychology principles, Human Art helps the user identify and develop a unique personal design profile. From design theory, Human Art uses the elements of design, line, shape, texture, color and space, as well as the principles of design, movement, balance, emphasis and unity to support the concept of a design harmony. Human Art uses color theory to support the correct communication and application of pure chroma colors, tones, tints and shades. Human Art uses art theory to direct the process of combining the elements of design and color in order to identify and interpret an individual's unique design profile. Human Art utilizes and adds to the body of literature concerning personality color theory and art therapy concepts to interpret and illuminate personality traits, patterns and relating styles.

One of the primary discoveries which makes Human Art truly unique is the concept that color, line and movement correlate consistently across all species and in nature itself. (This provides yet more proof that none of this happened by accident.) These observations are empirically based and provide the foundation for the program. For example, the design harmonies presented in this book can be validated in the color, lines and movement seen in various landscapes, plant life and in the animal kingdom.

Because these concepts are consistent across all physical dimensions, the concepts and the methodology provide a stable theory and system to identify the appropriate lines, color, scale, texture and contrast for each person's individual design. This type of combination—what we will refer to as "design elements"—is known as a "design harmony." When each element is precisely measured and combined in an appropriate manner, harmony is achieved and a masterpiece emerges.

I AM

I am unique —

Distinctly me —

Unlike any other.

My identity is written

In the pattern of combined vibrations

Within my tiniest cell:

A pattern that exists nowhere outside of me

Exactly the same.

I leave part of myself on everything I touch

And beneath the soles of my feet wherever I walk.

I am a vibratory song —

A rainbow of color —

An original.

— Carole Coombs

Human Art is an adventure in self-discovery. The human form is a work of art. The colors, textures and lines (angle of jaw, line of nose, arch of eyebrows, length of limbs, etc.) are not separate and haphazard parts of the whole, but are related and belong together, exactly like nature's other creations: the oak tree, weeping willow, cherry blossoms, hibiscus…are you getting the picture? Just as the elements of a fine painting or superb sculpture communicate a particular quality or message to viewers, so does the composition of the human body. It is a finished canvas, marvelously ordered.

Human Art is dedicated to exploring and discovering the various elements of the body which combine and harmonize, defining the complete individual—an individual who communicates the truth about who he or she is through his or her own personal style. By understanding the artistry and organization of the human form's design elements, Human Art selects from hundreds of colors those which not only relate to and harmonize with the eye, hair and skin tones, but also reflect the entire human figure. Human Art organizes these colors into a personal color spectrum that brings into focus the various and seemingly contradictory elements of a particular body into a uniquely harmonizing whole. The color fan and other design elements actually become an abstract portrait of the individual, illuminating the beautifully unified and orderly qualities of nature's creation. When individuals discover (and comply with) the design elements that repeat and harmonize with their own, they are freed from the dictates of seasonal fashion, rigid rules of "good taste" and stereotyped design ideas. They are then empowered to happily create and develop their own visual statement and their own personal style.

Have you discovered your beauty? Can you define and describe it at this point? If asked, could you write down 50 or even 100 positive words that describe you? Many people cannot define their beauty or are uncomfortable trying. Some people can describe their beauty, but they still lack the ability to comprehend its full measure. Human Art gives you the tools to do so.

In everything around us there is either harmony or disharmony. You can define harmony through all of the senses (hearing, sound, touch, etc.). It is the way everything is organized. Harmony is emotional, physical, esthetic and spiritual.

Harmony is either right or it is wrong. If you build a house and put it together well, that is harmony. If it is chaotic, it is not harmonious. It's a mess and eventually will fall down.

Harmony is organization; disharmony is disorganization. That definition, however, does not include elements that are abstract. There is a harmony to that. Abstract harmony in music is jazz. Abstract art is still art, and abstract thinking is thinking outside of the box.

Emotional harmony is linked to the spiritual. When you are emotionally harmonizing, you are dealing with truth.

Harmony in nature is paradise. Disharmony in nature is when the elements collide in earthquakes, eruptions, etc.

It's very basic. Harmony is truth and disharmony is wrong. It is vital. All energy goes into either harmony or disharmony.

— Donna O. Kearney

What Is a HARMONY?

WE HAVE ALREADY DISCUSSED WHAT CONSTITUTES HARMONY. NOW, IF WE LOOK AT OUR INDIVIDUAL MAKEUP AND HOW WE WERE CAREFULLY PUT TOGETHER, WE FIND MANY ELEMENTS THAT REPEAT OR INTERCONNECT WITHOUT DISRUPTION. THAT IS HARMONY WITHIN OURSELVES.

Your greatness lies back in your own
harmony, your blueprint,
what you've been since birth.

Now think of yourself. Your original makeup is harmonious. That is the masterpiece. When you were born, you were true to your harmony. Even your little imperfections were a part of that harmony. Your entire being was and is a communication of who you are and what your own harmony communicates. You then grow up and others unfortunately take pieces of their harmony that work so well for them and try to impose them on you. This phenomenon is the first step to disharmony. It makes you, for some uncanny reason, think you should be the same as other people. Then society imprints on you some of its own ideas about what it considers harmonious—how you *have* to wear your hair, what your fingernails *should* look like, etc.—and you are off and running on your way to your own chaos and eruption.

Stop! Go back! Your greatness lies back in *your* harmony, *your* blueprint, what *you* have been since birth. When you stay true to that true imprint and build upon its principles in all areas—esthetically, emotionally, physically and visually—you come home. You rediscover your inherent beauty.

When you are true to that beauty, people will instinctively recognize, or feel, your harmony. You were planned and created with that kind of truth. Don't abandon what you were intended to be. Find yourself again. Reorganize your harmony to truth. If you have already discovered it, build higher and higher levels of harmony or truths.

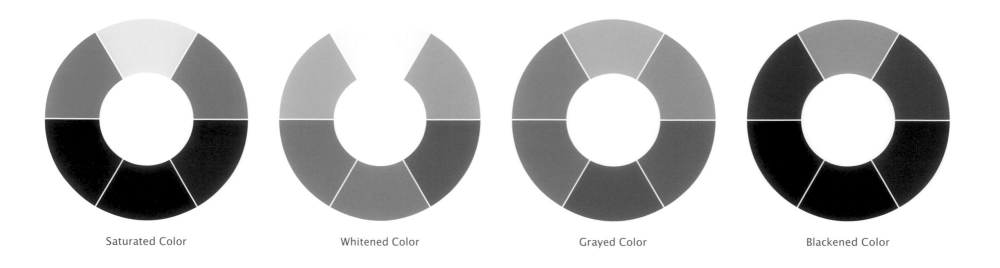

Saturated Color   Whitened Color   Grayed Color   Blackened Color

PRIMARY DESIGN ELEMENTS & HOW THEY CORRELATE

The Element of Color

As mentioned, Human Art deals with the primary design principles of color, line, sound and movement. Color is the type of color wheel that you relate to best, or that best harmonizes with you. That means you look good and feel good in these colors and you probably find that you surround yourself with them. These colors are a way to recognize who you are. Think of it this way: if you paint a painting or design anything, you start with the color wheel that best suits the type of ambiance you are trying to create. If you are going for simple and precise, or contemporary, you use what we call saturated colors. These hues are all the colors around the color wheel with nothing else added to them: pure red, pure green, pure yellow, etc.

If you want an animated design, you use whitened color. That is, you splash white into the saturated color wheel. By mixing with white, the colors become more animated, fun and youthful.

If you want elegant and refined, you carefully stir in gray. The gray mutes the color and adds elegance and mystique.

And if you want a rich, rustic and natural design, then you dump black into the saturated color wheel. Black adds depth and richness to the colors.

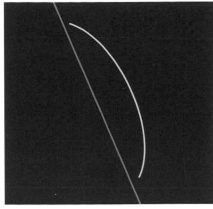

Saturated Lines   Whitened Lines   Grayed Lines   Blackened Lines

The Element of Line

Once you have picked the preferred color wheel for the desired ambiance, you then need to use its correlating lines in order to stay in its harmony. For example, if you are using saturated color, the correlating lines are oval, fast diagonal or parallel lines. These lines aren't "busy." They don't convey a sense of movement. Rather, they create the feeling of stillness. They are simple and create a contemporary look. The saturated lines and color create a saturated harmony.

When you are using the whitened color wheel, the correlating lines are circles or parts of circles and repetition. These lines communicate an animated ambiance and create youthfulness and liveliness.

For the grayed color wheel, the correlating line is the elongated "S" curve. This shape creates grace, elegance and length. It is languid, mystical and refined.

Finally, the blackened color wheel's correlating lines are angles or geometric shapes, which bring to mind things that are purposeful, rugged and natural.

The Elements of Sound & Movement

Saturated sound and movement is authoritative and still. It is aloof and standoffish.

Whitened sound and movement is bubbly and buoyant. It is slapstick and silly.

Grayed sound and movement is slow and graceful. It is soft and elegant.

Blackened sound and movement is deliberate and purposeful. It is natural and rich.

When you put all these elements together in each of the designs, you get a feeling of harmony that is consistent in, well, *everything*. You see these harmonies in nature, in animals and in people.

SATURATED

You see the saturated design in the mountaintops of the variety pictured in the accompanying illustration. Picture the snow-capped top of a majestic mountain, with the high contrast of the dark green pine trees against the white snow. Notice the fast diagonal of the top of the mountain with the parallel lines in the pine needles. These mountains are majestic, authoritative, motionless and intimidating. You also see the saturated design in the black panther. His movements are very precise and still. His nose, eyes and paws are oval shaped. He relates to the saturated harmony.

People who relate to the saturated harmony are authoritative. They move precisely, but are mostly still. When they walk, they stand tall and their limbs are motionless. They speak very properly and clearly. Their bone structure is consistent with the lines of the saturated harmony. Often, the bones in their face relate to ovals or are straight like parallel lines. Their fingers oftentimes are the same width all the way down the finger, which also relates to parallel lines. The mountaintops, the black panther and a contemporary piece of art, among many other things, have the same communication because they relate to the saturated harmony.

WHITENED

You'll find the whitened harmony in the mountain valleys and meadows, with the rolling hills and spontaneous flowers popping up. A common tree in the valleys is a quaking aspen. Its leaves are circles. The valleys have a feeling of youthfulness and spontaneity. The stream that runs through the valleys bubbles and dances; it imbues a feeling of movement and freshness. An animal that relates to this harmony is a bunny rabbit. It bounces, hops and moves buoyantly. Its body is made up of circles. It's cute and animated. God must have purposely left the bunny's voice in heaven—just imagine if it vociferated at the same rate its little nose moves! People who relate to the whitened harmony are animated as well. They talk a lot. They are spontaneous, lively and fun. Their bone structure relates to circles; you can see roundness (I'm talking about shape here—not size) in their faces. Their hands often look like a child's youthful hands.

The valleys, the bunny rabbit and the animated person all relate to the whitened harmony.

GRAYED

In nature, you find the grayed harmony in the swamps. I'm not referring to the mosquito-and alligator-infested stagnant pools of algae you see in bad cartoons. I'm thinking of the languid, romantic combination of slow-moving water and lush vegetation at twilight. The swamps I envision are mystical and elegant. A common tree in the swamps is a weeping willow. Its leaves are an elongated "S" curve. The feeling is refined and elegant. An animal that relates to this harmony is the afghan dog. It moves gracefully and relates to length. People who relate to this harmony are long and graceful. Their movements are languid and lissome. They are not rushed. They talk poetically, using very descriptive words.

The swamps, the afghan dog and the grayed person all fall into the grayed harmony.

Grayed

BLACKENED

You see the blackened harmony in the plateau regions. There, you find rustic shapes and colors, and you see and feel a rich earthiness when you experience them. The plateaus are bold and deliberate. An oak tree is blackened as well. It has a thick, no-nonsense trunk, and its leaves are angular. Animals that relate to the blackened harmony include tigers and lions. They are very deliberate. They move purposefully and sometimes abruptly. People who relate to the blackened harmony are also deliberate and can be abrupt. They are natural—you get what you see. You can hear them walk and move. You can even hear when they sit down because they will plop, rather than float, onto a chair. Their bone structure has angles and is very defined. Their bones communicate strength. The plateaus, the lion and the blackened person all relate to the same harmony: blackened. They all communicate the same feeling.

It is important to understand that we *all* relate to *all* these harmonies, but to varying degrees. They are present in order within us, and almost everybody will have a first, or most predominant harmony.

Blackened

THE LAW OF HARMONY WITHIN HARMONY

Human Art stems from many works and principles. One of the most significant is "Bel Viso," written by Carole Coombs and Donna Boam. This work identifies and uses the four basic classifications of color. These classifications are based on the work of the Nobel-prizewinning scientist, Wilhelm Ostwald. His theories are also validated by Faber Birren's classifications of color wheels when he established hue, tints, tones and shades. In all these works, the one common thread is the fundamental desire to establish harmony within harmony on every level. We all seem to crave this phenomenon of harmony within harmony. We strive for it in our surroundings, our appearance and everything we do. So, when we repeat the lines and colors of our individual harmony in our clothing, hair, houses, cars and general surroundings, we are more complete because we are validated by the way we look and feel.

Ostwald asserts, "The human form, like the rest of nature, is amazingly ordered." He's right. The beauty and harmony in nature results from its order. When we find our harmony, our order, we want to surround ourselves with and repeat it because we find our own design very soothing. This immersion in our own lines, color, sound and movement is like the complex layer of instruments in an orchestra. As each instrument chimes in one at a time, it adds a new depth, and eventually leads to the completeness and climax of a final song. We internalize it and it soothes us. When we first recognize our harmony, we can easily become engrossed, and the mere descriptions of it can cause an emotional awakening. See if you have an emotional reaction to, or deep-rooted recognition of, any of the following descriptions.

Polar bear in
  northern lights

The Four Harmonies & Their Natural Descriptions

Saturated

- Stark contrast of a winter landscape (dark green pine tree against white snow)
- Sharp definition
- Repeated lines
- Crystal clear icicles
- Row of slender cypress mirrored in still pools
- Silhouette of Manhattan skyline at dusk
- Parthenon crowning the Acropolis
- Stately Greek columns
- Gleaming marble
- White silk
- Sleek curve of the polar bear
- Steep, snow covered slopes
- Crescent moon
- Stained glass windows
- Orchids
- Bold, clear print
- Geisha
- High fashion
- Clean lines
- Long black cape
- Arched eyebrow
- A calculated turn of the head
- Aloofness
- Jacqueline Onassis
- Crystal, silver and white linen
- Transparent depths of an iceberg
- Chrome and glass
- Regal serenity

Whitened

- Force of life
- Sun's golden rays
- Rosebuds opening to the sun
- Uplifted and expectant faces of children
- Radiance
- Pulse of living
- Sense of wonder and inquiry
- Eagerness to participate
- Discovery, adventure, exploration
- Impetuous expectancy
- White layers of dogwood, blue sky, white clouds
- Cherry trees in a burst of pink
- Movement—spontaneous and light
- Restless, brisk, surging spiritedness
- Clip-clop syncopation of horses' hooves on cobblestone walks
- Baskets filled with cherries, apples and pears
- Children splashing in a puddle
- Puppies at play
- Living green meadows
- Painted eggs
- Wind teasing a paper down a hill
- The circus, Coney Island and Disneyland
- Marilyn Monroe
- The growth force, nurturing, accepting, sharing
- Energy
- Involvement
- Stimulating, elastic, exhilarating buoyancy
- Lightness and laughter

Grayed

- Glimpse of life as from under the sea: serene, diffused and enchanted
- Light coming through the forest, filtered and strained
- Solitary manor seen through mist on the moor
- Haze and melancholy of a wind-swept seashore
- Rainbow, diaphanous and ethereal
- Tender brown doe eyes, glimpsed through the leaves
- Misty otherworldliness of Merlin's forest
- Moss-hung trees by quiet ponds
- Relaxed quietude
- Subtle colors, grayed, blended, muted, shadowy and interwoven
- Jimmy Stewart
- Ink-washed Chinese painting
- Mauve afterglow of sunset
- Cool green dusk
- Impressionist painting, pale and soft
- Abalone shell
- Delicately-colored porcelain figure
- Iridescent opal and mother-of-pearl
- Heather and the full-blown rose
- Gossamer butterfly wings
- Sea grass moving in silky undulation: flowing, cascading and fluid
- Willows waving in a breeze
- Continuous curve of a gray Maserati
- Floating boas of ostrich feathers
- Gently winding stream
- Gilded opulence of a Louis XV drawing room: formal, soignée, and refined
- Soft hats and chiffon scarves

Blackened

- Earthy colors, deep and rich
- Mellowed terra cotta
- Copper bowls, clay vessels
- Grasses—dry and woven
- Tall tree trunks, great old cedars
- Heavy-laden sheaves of grain
- Hand-rubbed leather, nubby tweed
- Tree bark, pine cones, granite, sandstone
- German castles, Stonehenge
- Walt Whitman
- Force of rushing water
- Sharp, swift line
- Dynamic, powerful intensity
- Niagara Falls
- Tension of opposing lines; the winds of war
- Massive metal sculpture
- Geometric design
- Navajo rugs and arrows
- Jagged, rocky mountain peaks
- Lightning bolt
- Jackhammer
- Brigham Young
- Charging bull
- Arnold Schwarzenegger
- Lion's mane
- Beethoven
- Ethnic, funky print
- Mexican pottery
- Grand Canyon

Once you understand these principles of harmony, you will take pleasure in recognizing them in everything around you. Take, for example, the wind. A saturated wind blows in precise gusts. It whips in with an authoritative feel and leaves a sense of stillness behind. A whitened wind blows in flurries. You see it more in the objects it moves around, as if in a dance: papers pirouetting across the ground, leaves surfing through the grass. Its movement is playful and nonthreatening. A grayed wind is mystical, you can't quite pinpoint where it is, but you sense it is close by, with its soft whisper and its gentle, intermittent caresses. Finally, the blackened wind is the one that deliberately picks up your garbage can and puts it through your front window. It's a tornado of air around you. My guess is that everybody who reads these different descriptions can think of at least one person who relates to each different type of wind. If you can, then you're starting to understand the different harmonies.

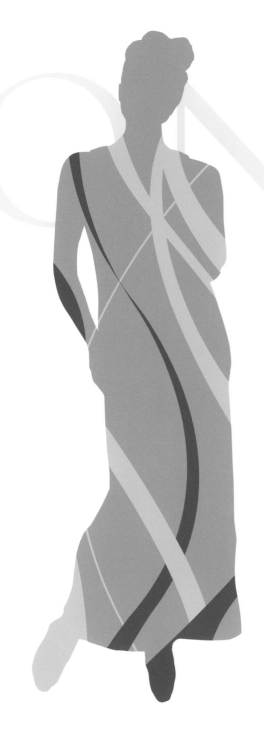

All these harmonies are made up of a family of characteristics we call designs. Human Art deals with four designs, just as art deals with four basic shapes. Two lines, straight and curved, make up these four basic shapes: circle, square, cone and cylinder. (Human Art also recognizes two versions of the cylinder that relate to Higgins gray and Emma saturation, which are simply shorter versions of the saturated and grayed designs). Any form comes from these four designs. The circle is animated. The square is angular. The cylinder is elongated and the cone is sleek. Similarly, Human Art harmonies consist of the four designs that convey the same feelings.

CHAPTER 3

The central focus for a saturated person
is competence and accuracy. She takes charge.

Saturated
HARMONY

PLEASE KEEP IN MIND AS YOU READ THE FOLLOWING SECTIONS THAT
ALTHOUGH I USE PRIMARILY FEMALE EXAMPLES, ALL THESE HARMONIES AND
THEIR CHARACTERISTICS APPLY EQUALLY TO BOTH SEXES AND ALL CULTURES.

The saturated harmony originates from all the colors on the color wheel in their pure form,
with no other color added to them. We refer to these colors as pure hues. The feeling you get
when surrounded by these colors is contemporary, precise and still.

$\mathcal{K}$ara is very saturated. When she walks in the door she stands tall and erect. She speaks very properly and communicates very clearly. She will greet people by saying something like, "Good morning," in a very diplomatic tone. She will then sit down, not wanting a lot of attention drawn to her. Just looking at her, you can't help but feel that she was put on this earth to take charge. Yet she is restrained; she doesn't want to make a scene. She often feels like she intimidates people, and sees this quality as negative. She therefore tries to be more approachable but finds her efforts ineffective.

Her beauty is striking. She has very light skin and dark hair. The lines in her body are straight, like a contemporary piece of furniture. She seems to get from one place to another without actually moving. The less she moves, the more you understand her and what she communicates. She is a very fine piece of art: simple, yet quality.

Kara relates to pure chroma color, which is color in its true form. As I began taking her around the color wheel, or as we call it, "pulling her colors," a very clear picture started to emerge. She is saturated, which means she also relates to very simple lines and smooth texture.

Her colors and lines tell me about her personality. They say, "Kara is a clear thinker. She is an organizer (though not always organized), she knows how to effectively delegate, and she is a perfectionist."

Saturated

We innately recognize these people
and surroundings because,
when exposed to them,
we automatically stand
a little straighter
or sit up in our chairs.
Even when describing
these elements we become quiet.

We have the same reaction
when we walk into a black tie event:
it demands our respect.

SATURATED	
COLOR	Hues, pure chroma color (crayon box)
LINE	Oval and straight body shapes, parallel lines, fast diagonal
CONTRAST VALUE	High
VISUAL FEATURES	Striking, sculptured, dramatic, serious, regal, polished
PERSONALITY	Competent, capable, efficient, aloof, private, intimidating, sophisticated, disciplined, influential
CAN BE	Uncompromising
THOUGHT PROCESS	Left brained, logical, decisive, clear thinker
SOUND	Authoritative, articulate, stately, advanced vocabulary
MOVEMENT	Still, minimal, controlled, sleek, precise
SCALE	Large features and bones
TEXTURE	Smooth, stiff, shiny
YANG	Broad shoulders, tall, stately, large, clear-cut features, erect, bold

CHAPTER 4

The central focus for a whitened person
is to have fun through understanding
and connecting with others.

Whitened
HARMONY

YOU ACHIEVE THE WHITENED HARMONY WHEN
YOU SPLASH WHITE INTO THE SATURATED COLOR
WHEEL. THE RESULTING COLORS ARE WHAT WE
REFER TO AS TINTS.

*B*rittany is whitened. When she walks through the door she bounces. One does not generally need to greet her, because she is already greeting everyone else. She is warm and social. If she sits in a chair, she does not sit very long; she moves from side to side or changes positions every few minutes. She relates to circles and animation. She is buoyant and talks with her hands. Youthfulness is her inherent beauty.

Brittany is like the sunshine coming into a room—she brightens it up. She is youthful no matter what her age. She is vibrantly alive and she often creates enthusiasm and makes things fun. She is social and everyone is important to her. She has no guile. She loves change and spontaneity. Her primary purpose is to experience fun and joy. She is youthful in her actions even when she is mature in years. You wouldn't be surprised to find her out roller-skating at the age of 103.

Whitened

Innocence is the beauty
of the whitened design.
We can't help but be happy
and laugh when in the company
of a whitened person.

WHITENED	
COLOR	Tints, warm coloring
LINE	Circles or parts of circles, repetition
CONTRAST VALUE	Low to medium
VISUAL FEATURES	Youthful, natural, animated, inviting, cheerful
PERSONALITY	Extroverted, lighthearted, spontaneous, bubbly, high energy, silly, childlike, cute
CAN BE	Noncommittal
THOUGHT PROCESS	Takes in information very quickly, spontaneous, nonstructured, nonconforming, unassuming, trusting, comforting
SOUND	Constant, rapid speech, giggly
MOVEMENT	Bouncing, active, busy, animated, maximum amount of movement
SCALE	Small features and bones
TEXTURE	Crisp, lightweight, decorated, soft
YANG	Small features, small bones, dainty, fragile, rounded, petite

The central focus for a grayed person
is to be appropriate. These people study
the details and process all contingencies.

Grayed HARMONY

THE GRAYED HARMONY APPEARS WHEN YOU CAREFULLY STIR GRAY INTO THE

SATURATED COLOR WHEEL. WE REFER TO THE RESULTING COLORS AS TONES.

Kate is grayed. She floats, rather than walks, in the door. Everything about her is graceful. For instance, she even sits in an "S" curve. Some view that posture as slouching, but I see it as melting into a chair. She is often soft spoken and detail oriented. She processes everything and sometimes finds it hard to make decisions. She can tend to get overwhelmed.

Her beauty is elegant. Her skin, features and hair are monochromatic, and she is very refined. She doesn't like to be the center of attention in a crowd; in fact, she would prefer to blend in instead of stand out.

As I took her around the color wheel I saw all the colors on the color wheel, just muted with gray. I could immediately see that she was very refined and dreamy.

Kate relates to an "S" curve that is elongated. Everything about her is elongated and drawn out. When she talks, everything flows. She will process her information over and over, in order not to leave anything out. Oftentimes, she doesn't like change.

Kate has an imprint that calms people. When she talks, she sounds like a flowing waterfall. Her words elegantly cascade over a mountain of adjectives. She mesmerizes us as she talks in her descriptive manner.

Grayed

*The grayed design
brings a refinement
and a grace to the earth;
whenever we see
these elements
we slow down
and experience life.*

GRAYED	
COLOR	Tones, cool coloring
LINE	Curved lines, elongated and "S" curved body shapes
CONTRAST VALUE	Medium
VISUAL FEATURES	Dignified, subtle, elegant, mysterious, delicate, refined, distinctive
PERSONALITY	Introverted, soft spoken, diplomatic, empathetic, proper, meticulous, preferring to observe rather than participate
CAN BE	Indecisive
THOUGHT PROCESS	Complex, idealistic, sensitive, worrying, nurturing, artistic, peacemaker, intuitive, sentimental
SOUND	Eloquent, articulate, reserved, minimal, small voice
MOVEMENT	Graceful, languid, flowing
SCALE	Small, medium and large features
TEXTURE	Soft, limp, billowy, sheer, matte, dull, fine quality, expensive
YANG	Feminine, refined, elongated

CHAPTER 6

*The central focus for a blackened person
is to get the job done. These people are very task
oriented and build much of what we see around us.*

Blackened
HARMONY

THE BLACKENED HARMONY ORIGINATES WHEN YOU DUMP BLACK INTO THE

SATURATED COLOR WHEEL. WE REFER TO THE RESULTING COLORS AS SHADES.

Blackened

*J*eanie is blackened. She strides through the door with a mission and states her purpose. She is results-driven. For instance, if she doesn't like a wall in her house, she gets a bulldozer and knocks it down. She will then build a new one. She takes problems head on and deals with them with the intent to solve them as quickly as possible. She believes in getting things done and moving on.

Jeanie is very honest and direct. She speaks as deliberately as she moves and she tells it like it is. She is the one who would approach you to tell you that you have spinach in your teeth when everyone else is pretending not to notice. Her intentions would be good—she would tell you out of an honest desire to help solve the problem. Although often blunt, blackened people are at heart very kind.

She relates to angles; you see them in her body and her face. Her beauty is natural and exotic. She loves sports and the outdoors. Blackened people love nature.

In this and the previous descriptions, you'll notice I make mention of "contrast value." Contrast value is a very important concept; it is how we measure the harmony of light to dark within one's design. It is also an important clue about the level of authoritativeness in one's harmony. If someone's contrast value is high, she relates to the boldness of light to dark, and she is also a very authoritative person. If a person's contrast value is low, she relates to light to dark in a less authoritative, softer way, just as she has a "softer" personality. An example of contrast value is the darkness of someone's natural hair color, eyebrows or eyelashes compared to the lightness of his or her skin.

*The blackened design
and traits are wonderful.
These people just seem to know
how to deal with life.
They also possess
a very natural attractiveness.
They are the ones
who look great sitting on a rock,
wearing leather,
while the wind blows
through their hair.*

BLACKENED	
COLOR	Shade, warm coloring
LINE	Angular body shapes, vertical lines forming right angles, diagonal lines or intersecting lines, geometric patterns
CONTRAST VALUE	Medium to high
VISUAL FEATURES	Bold, rough, defined, physical, large muscle, strong, powerful, casual, earthy
PERSONALITY	Assertive, direct, confident, structured, informal, practical, efficient, stable, conservative
CAN BE	Overbearing
THOUGHT PROCESS	Task-oriented, compartmentalized
SOUND	Loud, raspy, rough, deep
MOVEMENT	Deliberate, medium
SCALE	Large features and bones
TEXTURE	Rough, nubby, natural, thick, matte, dull
YANG	Angular, tough, athletic, sturdy

CHAPTER 7

Design ELEMENTS

THE DESIGN ELEMENTS WE WILL FOCUS ON FOR THE SAKE OF EASY RECOGNITION ARE THOSE THAT PERTAIN TO COLOR, LINE, SOUND AND MOVEMENT. COLOR AND LINE ARE VERY COMMON AND EASY TO RECOGNIZE. SOUND AND MOVEMENT ARE A LITTLE MORE DIFFICULT TO PINPOINT. THE ELEMENTS OF DESIGN WE PULL FROM ARE THE EMPIRICAL ONES: THE ONES WE ARE USED TO SEEING EVERY DAY. SPECIFICALLY, WE CONCENTRATE OUR ATTENTION WHERE COLOR, LINE, SOUND AND MOVEMENT MEET.

The two basic lines are straight and curved.

Faber Birren writes, "Science is essentially intellectual; art is essentially emotional." I would add that because the elements of design are empirical, we have been able to organize and combine both art and science. The science of color, line, sound and movement is both intellectual and emotional.

In art, the interpretation of what is beautiful swings like a pendulum. During one era, a certain communication seems to dominate, and its opposite will gain favor in a different era. For example, in paintings from the Renaissance era, the women were soft, feminine and round. This line, or in this case, this type of body, personified the ultimate in beauty during that era. The communication of that type of line or body suggests nurturing femininity. I imagine many women and men were eating themselves sick or stuffing their clothes to obtain the desirable look of the age. However, when you look at magazine covers today, it appears that straight-boned, lean bodies personify the ultimate in beauty.

The interesting point is that both communications, at different times, have held the title of the most desirable, beautiful look. This begs the question, "Says who?" Society has limited our views about color, line, sound, movement and the value inherent in each different communication of beauty. This limited view simply makes no sense. When you paint, if you want the painting to look soft and nurturing, you use the lines that communicate that harmony. When you want it to look strong, you use different lines. In the end, both paintings are beautiful. The important point is that all the different communications are wonderful in their own right. And so are you!

PRIMARY & SECONDARY DESIGN ELEMENTS

Your primary design is your dominant design. You can recognize your dominant design by your initial response to a stimulus or by what you communicate to others right off the bat. The test I use the most is the scenario of, "What will you do if the door falls off?"

If you were at an establishment and the front door fell off, your first response to the situation would illustrate your tendencies, or your primary design.

The saturated people would stand up and announce, "The door fell off!" and would begin to delegate responsibilities to other people.

The whitened people would stand up and say excitedly, "Wow! The door fell off!" They would call their friends, laughing, and say, "You should have seen the door fall off. Get down here and bring a pizza. I'm not kidding, the door just up and fell right off."

The grayed people would say to themselves (not aloud), "The door fell off and it's near closing time. It will be difficult to get in touch with someone to come fix it, and it's supposed to rain. I wonder what caused it to fall off, anyway."

The blackened people would get up and put the door back on.

"WHAT WILL YOU DO IF THE DOOR FALLS OFF?"

"The door fell off!"

"Wow! The door fell off!"

"The door fell off and it's near closing time."

"I will fix it."

Your primary harmony is the one to which you are most drawn—the one that comes most naturally to you.

Your initial response is almost always indicative of your predominant design. Your primary harmony is the one to which you are most drawn—the one that comes most naturally to you. You surround yourself in elements from this harmony. Your personality communicates it. Oftentimes, you dress in this harmony, move in the manner of this harmony and even think in a way that relates to aspects and elements of this harmony.

However, nobody is so limited that he or she only communicates elements from one harmony. After a person's initial reaction, the following reactions tend to fall in order of design. For instance, a blackened person may get up and put the door back on, but if her secondary design is grayed, she might afterwards feel embarrassed and wonder how many people watched her do it and what they thought. The amount of each of the remaining designs that each person has will influence the predominant design.

If you were a client at Human Art, we would first, obviously, look at you, then we would talk to and listen to you and pull your best colors. By that time, we'd have a pretty good idea about what you'd do if the proverbial door fell off. Then we would pull your personality color fan. Your personality colors are the best projecting colors from each color family in your personal fan. We put these colors in order of the most projecting color to the least. We interpret the true intent, or meaning, of each color. From there, we add the influence of your design (order of harmonies) and *voila*—we have a very complete picture of you. The fan that we put together for you illuminates, in great detail, how you think and interact with people. It's a great aid in facilitating interpersonal skill and a truly unique equation, or measurement if you will, of how you were put together. No two fans have ever come out the same. Just a little different combination of one element or another can make you completely different from anyone else, even those with whom you see similarities.

THE PERSONAL DESIGN PROFILE ASSESSMENT

Within each of the four design categories (saturated, whitened, grayed and blackened), several dimensions need to be assessed in order to complete the personal design profile. The following items comprise the Personal Design Profile Assessment (PDPA):

1. Color: Different

PURE CHROMA, SHADES, TONES & TINTS

Clients relate to different colors. First we take a person all the way around the color wheel. Within each color (primary, secondary, tertiary) we find the right amount of saturation, white, gray and black that defines the combination of his or her design. We accomplish this objective by measuring the amounts of each of these harmonies and where they lie in order of projection and harmonious tones when held up to the person.

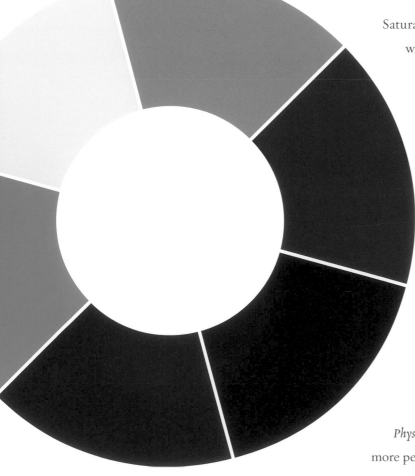

COOL COLORING

Saturated and grayed people relate to cool coloring and tend to be introverted. Introverts look within. They focus on what they are thinking and feeling and their actions revolve around that introspection. They have a very active inner world. If you are an introvert, much goes on within you that you don't share with others. In fact, you may rarely express yourself freely.

You are self-determined. In other words, your personal standards and evaluations of what is good and not good form the bottom line of your decisions. Others may perceive you as stubborn if they attempt to convince you of an idea or action that conflicts with your own inner standards or convictions. You may suffer much inner pain when you violate your own standards. You have high integrity. Change, or breaking traditions, is difficult for you. You tend to be conservative.

You are good at concentrating on and dealing with tasks which require attention to detail. Others may perceive you, or you may perceive yourself, as a perfectionist. Sedentary pursuits such as reading, writing, music, study, art, bookkeeping or careful handwork—small muscle activity—are pleasurable to you. You like a calming, tranquil environment.

Physical activity: You prefer individual sports over contact or team sports. You have a need for more personal space. You need some comfort, cleanliness and order.

Social: You enjoy sedentary leisure: reading, musical instruments, theatre, etc. You enjoy small groups of close friends or family versus large groups and parties. Confusion and noise can make you uncomfortable. You are very loyal and committed to partner, family and friends. You are reserved, often shy.

Service and work: You are good at planning, ideas and organization. You are able to work alone and are observant of fine detail.

Opposite sex: You form strong attachments, and are loyal and committed to your partner. You need to know someone—and even admire him or her—before intimacy or physical contact. Unfaithfulness is a violation of your partnership that is hard to forgive. You are romantic and need to trust.

WARM COLORING

Whitened and blackened people relate to warm coloring and tend to be extroverted. Extroverts look outside themselves at the outer world. They are receptive and open to external influences. If you are an extrovert, you relate readily to your social environment. You express emotions openly and freely.

You are receptive to those around you and sometimes suggestible or easily engaged by the ideas and enthusiasm of others. Self-doubt or fear does not characterize you; you enjoy newness and change. You're bored by too much introspection and deliberating. You tend to be decisive and enjoy taking risks and meeting challenges. You may find rules to be restrictive.

You can become restless with sedentary tasks. You like motion, activity and strong physical exercise. You need to release energy with sports or large muscle activity.

Physical activity: You like team sports with rugged contact. You have less need for personal space. You also tend to be competitive. You can adjust to a rugged environment or conditions. You are adventuresome, even daring.

Social: You enjoy groups of people, excitement, parties, etc. You like physical contact. You are exhilarated and stimulated when a lot is going on.

Service and work: You're good at doing things and taking action. You are typically the one to say, "Let's stop talking about it and do something about it." You are energetic and forceful. You like and need to be with people and you prefer not to be alone for long. You are confident—a good salesperson and leader. You can be assertive.

Opposite sex: Lucky you! You are ardent and strongly attractive to others. You may be impatient with slow-paced romance. You like newness and change—it may take discipline for you to commit to one person. You are passionate and emotionally expressive.

2. Line: Shapes & Patterns

A line joins two points. That is a simple definition, yet the symbols that are extracted from this simplicity wield enormous power and communication. Since earliest times, man has used linear symbols for visual communication, yet we often don't clearly understand the response we feel to these symbols. The response is an instant one, which virtually bypasses the intellect and makes a powerful impact upon the emotions. Because this impact is so immediate, the effect is often a subliminal one, and the viewer might be intellectually unaware of his or her strong, emotional response. The person who understands the feelings and ideas communicated by these seemingly simple lines can process his or her responses to them more accurately and can also learn to use lines to more effectively communicate with others.

Understanding what a line is, is simple. Understanding what a line does is more difficult because of the subtlety of its communication. On the first level, lines indicate the shape of things and provide direction and movement for the eye. We enjoy observing lines in nature: the branching of trees, bubbles rising in water, smoke curling up from a fire, undulating wheat fields, jagged peaks, etc. Fine artists employ lines to express mood: calmness, excitement, aggression, etc. Similarly, lines on the human body—the arch of an eyebrow, the length of fingers, the shape of the jaw, communicate a great deal about a person. In the same way, linear elements added to the body—the shape of a hairstyle, the hem of a skirt, the design of a pocket, are visually significant. We want to duplicate the lines that are visible in our bone structure and facial features. Notice the lines of your eyebrows, nostrils, jawbone, hands and feet (ovals, fast diagonals, parallel lines, circles, "S" curves, right angles, geometric shapes, etc.). These lines are the pattern you should follow.

As stated earlier, only two types of lines exist: straight and curved. From each of these lines comes four basic shapes: the circle, square, cylinder and cone. You can use these four basic shapes to create many lines and forms. The important factor is how you use them and what message the combinations, or shapes, communicate. For instance, a curve can be very slight, which communicates one message, or move all the way to a complete circle, which creates a totally different feeling. Horizontal lines are calming because they suggest the quiet calm of the horizon or flat, resting water. Vertical shapes instill in us the feeling of stability, grandeur and the uprightness of a stately tree. Swirls and flows suggest languorous plant growth or the fascination of a rising flame. Rounded lines have a buoyant movement like soap bubbles bouncing and dancing in a breeze. Thus, when related to body or clothing design, the straight line is distinguished, static and calming; the rounded line suggests restlessness and quick movement; and the slight curve communicates restraint and moderation because it is constantly trying to become straight.

A line can cause the eye to move in any direction, even though it is one-dimensional. Each type of line communicates different kinds of movement. Vertical lines—forming right angels to the earth—are static and stable; horizontal lines are calm, at rest; diagonal lines or intersecting lines indicate powerful movement and activity; curved lines are graceful, undulating and flowing; and circles or parts of circles are animated and buoyant.

Because line communicates so strongly and because each human form is already composed of its own lines, angles and curves, adding the right lines to our bodies (e.g. makeup, hairstyles, clothing, etc.) is very important, because it communicates the same kinds of feelings and ideas. David Ruskin states our goal simply and beautifully:

One of the most important requirements of all art is that it conforms to the law of Unity Within Unity. Since the human body contains the most beautiful lines and forms, unity requires that we do not contradict this form . . . thus a good silhouette will be related to body structure—a balance between concealing and revealing. The wearer will be beautifully fused with his/her clothes.

— David Ruskin

Human Art is combining and organizing all these lines, shapes and patterns to make sense and tell the truth. Great artists understand how lines communicate. Now, you don't need a background in art to understand these principles as well. You can now enjoy your own beauty and also know how to get along better with others, all because of the use or communication of a line. This principle is like a universal language that we have all been speaking, without even being aware of it. Once you understand it, you can communicate even more effectively.

Previously, we have used the analogy of an artist choosing the proper lines to portray a certain ambiance in his painting. As human beings, however, we don't pick the right lines for ourselves. We don't *apply* a particular communication; we already possess it. We can see this communication in the lines of our bones and limbs, and in the very shapes of our bodies and faces. All these lines manifest themselves naturally—we just need to look for and recognize them. It's amazing how we can look at our own faces and bodies so differently when we start understanding these principles. As Teresa Jahuner, a corporate regional manager for Matrix says, "We are looking at things through a new pair of glasses."

3. Lines & Color

The lines and shapes in our bone structures, eyes, eyebrows, lips, etc. also correspond in an amazing way to our type of coloring. The colors and shapes of our bodies belong together.

1. Oval and straight body shapes and lines will be found with human coloring that relates to pure chroma colors: bold, highly saturated colors.

2. Rounded body shapes and lines will be found with coloring that relates to whitened colors or tints.

3. Elongated and oval body shapes and lines will be found with coloring that relates to grayed colors or tones.

4. Angular body shapes and lines will be found with coloring that relates to blackened colors or shades.

To the extent that a person's bone structure varies from the prototype, his or her coloring will also vary. Remember, we all possess a combination and variation of design elements, but the most dominant design theme is easily discernible and important to understand if the colors and lines we add to our body are to harmonize with what already exists in us.

We all possess a combination and variation of design elements.

Eyes

SATURATED

- Smooth
- Oval
- Sculptured
- Symmetrical

WHITENED

- Round
- Button shaped
- Bright, youthful

GRAYED

- End of the eye extends or is drawn out like a sleepy or dreamy eye
- There is a slight "S" curve to the eye lid

BLACKENED

- Angular, small angles around the eye in various places

Lips

SATURATED

- Smooth, like it has been precisely sculptured and then smoothed over
- Although lips tend to be thinner on the edge and full in the middle they still possess a symmetrical feeling

WHITENED

- Pouty, soft, voluptuous with an innocent, natural fullness

GRAYED

- Edges slightly drawn out or down
- Soft in a dreamy manner

BLACKENED

- Visible angles, strong
- Often times (convex) which creates an angle on the silhouette

Noses

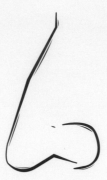

SATURATED

- Strong yet smooth, straight or oval arch
- Bones are often parallel or end with an oval
- Strong symmetry
- Nostrils oval

WHITENED

- Button nose turned up
- Nostrils round

GRAYED

- "S" curve as bone cascades down
- Lengthy yet softly refined
- Nostrils "S" curve or sometimes paisley shaped

BLACKENED

- Strong chiseled angles and natural bumps
- Nostrils angular

Chins

SATURATED

- Smooth
- Oval
- Precise

WHITENED

- Round, circular almost buoyant lines where jaw bones meet the chin

GRAYED

- Drawn down with length

BLACKENED

- Angular and square
- Strong and chiseled
- Often a cleft chin

Johannes Itten, whose work and case studies form part of the foundation for our work in Human Art, said:

He who wants to become a master of color must see, feel and experience each individual color in its many endless combinations with all other colors. Colors must have a mystical capacity for spiritual expression, without being tied to objects.

Color effects are in the eye of the beholder. Yet the deepest and truest secrets of color effect are, I know, invisible even to the eye, and are beheld by the heart alone. The essential eludes conceptual formulation.

Students often ask this question, and my answer is always the same: If you, unknowing, are able to create masterpieces in color, then acknowledge is your way. But if you are unable to create masterpieces in color out of your acknowledge, then you ought to look for knowledge.

Knowledge of the laws of design need not imprison, it can liberate from indecision and vacillating perception. What we call laws of color, obviously, can be no more than fragmentary, given the complexity and irrationality of color effects.

Color is life; for a world without colors appears to us as dead. Colors are primordial ideas, children of the aboriginal colorless light and its courtyard, colorless darkness. As flame begets light, so light engenders colors. Colors are the children of light, and light is their mother. Light, that first phenomenon of the world, reveals to us the spirit and living soul of the world through colors.

Colors are forces, radiant energies that affect as positively or negatively, whether we are aware of it or not.

Whether we know it or not, all of us are continually responding to the special qualities of the visual elements. Our minds may be focused on other, more practical, matters as we move from place to place with great efficiency during our working days. But what many of us do not realize is that the pattern of the whole visual field is working on us all the time. Not only what we are momentarily focusing upon, but the entire surrounding field, to the limits of our peripheral acuity, is continuously making its impression on us. And, most often, without our knowing this at all, we respond to this total configuration of visual stimuli.

What else is it but the effect of the whole visual field that causes us to feel at ease in one house and uneasy in another? True, the inhabitants of the houses, by the particular quality of their presence, may contribute in one way or another to an overriding degree; but what if the houses are without occupants? Then it is the composite effect of colors, sizes, shapes and textures in relation to ourselves which either invites or turns us away. And the same is true for landscape. We are caused to experience feelings of one sort when what lies around us are the huge, jagged, pyramidical shapes and the blue-gray color of the High Sierras, and feelings of quite another sort when we find ourselves to be the most vertical shape on the almost unbroken tan-white flatland of the Gulf of Texas. In either case, these special configurations of visual qualities get to us. So long as our eyes are open, they work to activate us in mind and body and thereby let us know in tacit ways where we are and how we are in relation to what is around us. We can say that the visual elements, in and of themselves, play this expressive role in all of our lives.

It is impossible with words to show how all these quite different things exist together in a particular pattern having a particular quality as a whole.

— Johannes Itten

In other words, color is difficult to define. But while the concrete *definition* may be elusive, I submit that the *laws* of design and color are empirical and organized. Color is defined by the reaction it evokes, and this reaction varies from person to person. The same can be said of lines. When we see a line, we react to it. We feel the same communication when we they see an elegant silk scarf flowing in the wind as we do when we see a woman whose body lines seems to float as she walks to a chair and melts into it, slouching as if to conform to the chair. Both pictures have the same elements and the same emotional effect on us.

Contrast the previous picture to a boulder falling down a slope. Its movement is deliberate, dramatic and visually arresting—you feel compelled to watch. You hear it each time it hits the ground. When a person with the same kinds of lines walks into a room, he paints a similar picture. He catches your attention, and you hear each of his steps hit the floor. He walks very purposefully, as if he has something important to which he must immediately attend. These two pictures communicate the same beauty. When we observe the different kinds of lines and their movements, we feel completely different emotions—it's observable. We understand this effect on a subconscious level, we just need to be more aware of it on a conscious level, so we can readily recognize and happily acknowledge all the different kinds of beauty.

4. Scale

Scale relates to the size of features and bones. Achieving balance with scale in mind is very important. For instance, people who relate strongly to the saturated design usually have larger features and bones. Therefore, tiny, dainty or wispy pieces of jewelry on saturated people would look inharmonious—sort of like putting ketchup on a hot fudge sundae. Each design has its own scale, which can impact everything from fabric patterns to tie width.

5. Movement

Movement has to do with vibrations sent through the eye to the brain. Vibrations are minimal when color is solid and surfaces are smooth and flat. Vibrations increase with the increase of warm colors, patterns, folds and textures on a surface. We recognize movement when we observe it in the way people walk and talk—even how they sit, etc. Movement manifests itself through individuals and relates to their harmony as well.

Hairlines

SATURATED

- Clean
- Symmetrical
- Often a widow's peak

WHITENED

- Nonstructured

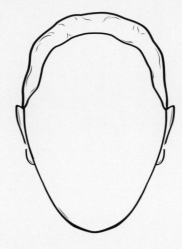

GRAYED

- Blended not exaggerated

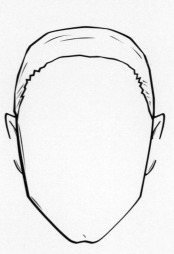

BLACKENED

- Square
- Often low forehead

Hands

SATURATED

- Same width all the way down the fingers, promoting parallel lines
- Oval or parallel nail beds
- Smooth texture of skin

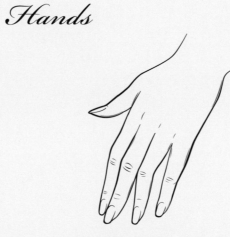

WHITENED

- Childlike, angelic, young fleshy soft texture
- Tapers at the end of fingers
- Short fingers

GRAYED

- Lengthy, tapered fingers
- Lengthy palms
- Delicate or softly refined
- Often "S" curves as fingers taper down

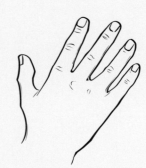

BLACKENED

- Strong, square with naturally leathered texture
- Square nail beds and angular nails
- Thick appearance and rough texture to the skin

Movement of Hair

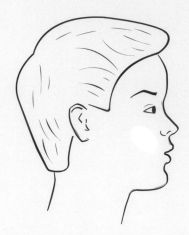

SATURATED

- Smooth
- Still
- Minimal movement

WHITENED

- Often curly but can be straight
- Tousled and free

GRAYED

- Refined movement
- Blended, meticulous but not stiff
- Length is important or the illusion of length when hair is shorter

BLACKENED

- Volume
- Messy
- Curly or straight
- Angles, spikes

Hairstyles

SATURATED

- Classic
- Dramatic
- High fashion

WHITENED

- Fun
- Change
- Free
- Childlike and friendly

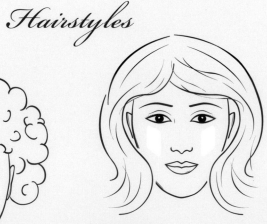

GRAYED

- Elegant
- Refined flowing

BLACKENED

- Exotic
- Natural
- Bold
- Low maintenance

A person's thought process relates to movement also. A saturated client's thoughts are still and precise. A whitened person's thoughts are quick and spontaneous. A grayed person's thoughts are slow and methodical, and a blackened person's thoughts are abrupt and deliberate. People's thoughts correlate with their inherent harmony, which is a magnificent thing to observe. You can work backwards as well: if someone displays the lines of a particular harmony, you can count on him thinking and moving in the same manner.

6. Texture

Texture includes everything three dimensional about design. (i.e. soft, stiff, smooth, silky, rough, nubby, shiny, etc.)

7. Sound

Sound refers to volume, or whether a person is loud or soft-spoken. The sound a person usually emits is also indicative of her design. For example, a saturated person whose harmony is still will often speak in a still manner. When you listen to her, her voice sounds proper and precise. A whitened sound is animated—whitened people talk fast and their words sound bouncy. A grayed voice is languid and calming. The blackened sound is deliberate and abrupt.

8. Looks & Visual Features

People's overall presentations appear striking, polished, youthful, natural, animated, dignified, delicate, bold, rough, etc., according to their predominant design. (See Personal Design Profile Assessment on page 102.)

9. *Personality Style & Thinking Process*

An individual's personality style and thinking process determine whether she is competent, private, logical, introverted, a peacemaker, etc. We call this aspect of Human Art "the brains."

Saturated

Saturated people think in black and white—not gray. They make a decision and that is the final answer. They have the ability to take a lot of information and quickly figure out what is important and what is not. They can sometimes be all-or-nothing thinkers.

Whitened

Whitened people think very quickly and spontaneously. Because of the fact that they process information so quickly, others tend to think they do not think things through. Whitened people can sometimes interrupt because they process thoughts so much faster than other people do. They can also concentrate on multiple tasks at one time. However, whitened people may tend to leave tasks unfinished simply because they lose interest in activities.

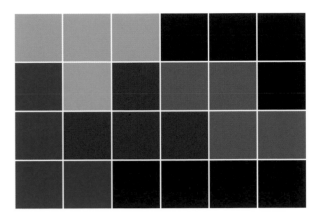

BLACKENED

The blackened thinking process is compartmentalized. Blackened individuals put their day together in boxes that carefully fit together, and then they open them one at a time in a logical order. They tend to get agitated if you pull one of the boxes out of place by being late or doing anything that throws them off schedule.

GRAYED

Grayed people's thinking is a continuous processing activity. Their thoughts go on and on, interconnect, and lead them in many different directions. Grayed people have a flair for details—they are excellent to have on planning committees. They leave no stone unturned, which can also lead them to worry, sometimes about things that do not happen.

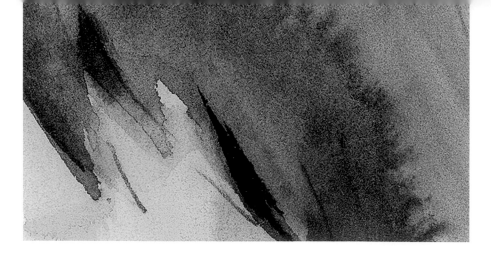

Human Art claims that personality and thought processes are additional elements in the overall personal design picture, and they, too, are empirically based. In other words, personality features have been observed over the years to consistently occur and cluster with the other design elements. Historically, psychologists have developed many approaches to help categorize clusters of personality traits. Perhaps the most common approach was the concept of the archetype. Simply stated, an archetype is the original model after which all other similar persons are patterned, copied or emulated. As in Jungian psychology, an archetype can be described as a thought and behavioral pattern that finds worldwide parallels and acceptance. For example, Jung described the following archetypes:

- The Syzygy (Divine Couple)*
- The Child
- The Superman
- The Hero
- The Great Mother
- The Wise Old Man
- The Trickster

*Carl Jung referred to the syzygy as a concept denoting the symbolic integration of opposites into one whole, as evidenced by the union of heaven and earth, spirit and matter, masculinity and femininity. The concept signifies the harmony and balance between the various opposing qualities that make up the psyche.

As a result of Carl Jung's work, the interest in personality typing started to gain momentum. In an effort to make Carl Jung's theories operational, Isabel Myers and Katherine Briggs developed the MBTI. The MBTI is a personality typing inventory which measures an individual's preference for the following four personality traits:

- EXTRAVERSION VS. INTROVERSION: This dichotomy indicates how people view the world around them and whether they are energized by others and their surroundings or prefer to address the inner world of ideas and concepts.

- SENSING VS. INTUITION: This dichotomy considers how the individual takes in information—through concrete sensing or the more abstract method of intuition.

- THINKING VS. FEELING: This third dichotomy indicates how individuals use information when making decisions. The more logical and objective method is referred to as the "thinking" function and is preferred by 60 percent of males. The more value-related and subjective method is referred to as "feeling" and is preferred by 60 percent of women.

- JUDGING VS. PERCEIVING: These attitudes indicate how an individual organizes and operates in the outside world. The judging type will be systematic and decisive, while the perceiving type will be random and open-ended.

Personality features have been observed over the years to consistently occur and cluster with the other design elements.

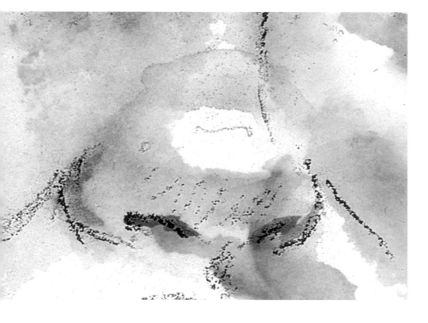

In addition to archetypes and personality typing, physiognomy/personology (face reading) has been around for 2500 years. This science of physiognomy has flourished since the time of the Greeks, amongst the Chinese and Indians, with the Romans, in the Arab world and during the European renaissance. Physiognomy faded in popularity during the 18th century, was eclipsed by phrenology in the 19th century, and has been resurrected by personologists in the 20th century.

Dr. Edward Vincent Jones, a United States Superior Court judge, coined the term personology in the mid-20th century. Dr. Jones, having dealt with thousands of court cases displaying every conceivable type of personality from genius to criminal, compiled a list of 200 physical traits that he was eventually able to confidently relate to human character and behavior. Over the years, Jones narrowed his list of physical traits to 68. The following list contains examples of some of the correlations Dr. Jones put forth:

- Coarse hair: less sensitive
- Fine hair: extremely sensitive
- Tight skin across frame of face: like things to be very clean and neat
- Wide jaw: likes to be in charge
- Square chin: loves to debate

While science continues to question the validity of categorizing people or imposing labels and stereotypes without a thorough clinical assessment, such theories have many useful applications in our interpersonal contacts and human relations. By understanding the core personality conflicts and how people vary from each other in very basic ways, archetypes, personality typing and even personology add to our body of interpersonal knowledge.

Among all these psychology fields, Human Art is unique because it is based on the concept of personal design elements, which are all observable and objective traits. Because we know which elements relate to each other, we can predict and cross-reference each trait or element. For example, when we observe oval and parallel lines; high contrast value; sculptured, dramatic and regal visual features; authoritative, articulate sound; and still, controlled, precise movement, we can predict a personality style marked by sophistication, competence, discipline and influence. The thought process will be left-brained, logical, decisive and clear thinking. Similarly, if a person displays circular lines and

parts of circles in their bone structure; medium value contrast; youthful, animated, inviting visual features; giggling, rapid sound; and bouncy, busy movement, we can predict a personality style that exhibits such qualities as spontaneity, childlike exuberance, extraversion and high energy. The accompanying thought processes would be nonstructured, nonconforming, unassuming and trusting.

Thus, if we know several dimensions or elements within a particular harmony, we can then predict with confidence the missing dimensions. (See the Personal Design Profile Assessment for a summary of the design elements for each harmony on page 102.) Once people are trained in the advanced levels of Human Art, they are able to diagnose the predominant design harmony and understand the varying degrees of all the design elements formulating each person's unique equation.

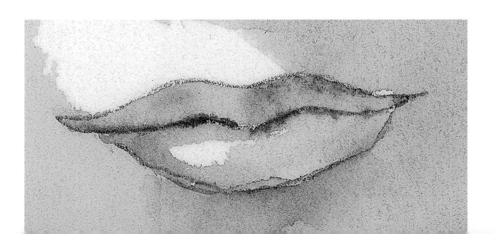

CHAPTER 8

Customer Service
by DESIGN

AS YOU CAN SEE, HUMAN ART BECOMES A POWERFUL TOOL IN HUMAN RELATIONS BECAUSE IT PROMOTES TOLERANCE FOR THE BASIC DIFFERENCES BETWEEN PEOPLE. IT ALSO PROVIDES AN UNOBTRUSIVE WAY TO QUICKLY ASSESS, WITHOUT GIVING A WRITTEN SURVEY, WHAT IS IMPORTANT TO OTHERS AND WHAT THEIR BASIC THOUGHT PROCESS AND CORE NEEDS WILL BE.

Prior to getting their colors pulled, most people we work with can't figure out why other people don't like dressing in their own particular taste or sense of style. All their lives they have been drawn to their own design. For example, a saturated person loves simple, sleek clothing lines and is drawn to the pure chroma colors. She cannot figure out why others may be drawn to what she considers garish outfits. When people understand that their particular style goes with their harmony, it really opens their eyes and helps them comprehend that they are uniquely drawn to what makes them most comfortable. Consequently, they also learn and accept that others are drawn to their own designs as well.

The same can be said about design thinking. We think and process according to our own harmony, and so do others. For instance, since the saturated and grayed designs are more introverted, they think inwardly and their world goes on inside their heads. Whitened and blackened people are extroverted, so their world happens and they verbalize it as they go. The introverted people might think the extroverts are obnoxious, or busybodies. On the other hand, the extroverted designs might think that their introverted counterparts are stuffy, conceited or even wimpy. When we start to understand the differences in the designs we allow for them, we celebrate each other rather than criticize.

One good example is a saturated person I know who was very critical of her friend because of the way that friend decorated her home. The saturated woman, of course, likes things simple and clinical. When she would see her friend's house she couldn't understand why it was so busy. It wasn't until her colors were pulled in Human Art that she understood that she innately loved things neat and unadorned, while her whitened friend innately loved a lot of movement. They were both expressing their built-in qualities. With their newfound knowledge, they reached a point of appreciation and acceptance and did not try to impose their own tastes on each other anymore. This acceptance was a very powerful breakthrough in their friendship.

Since each of the design elements is empirically based, each of us can quickly observe the people around us and decide how we will interact with them. Human Art strives to improve relationships through enhanced empathy and understanding of each other's basic design elements. At Human Art we call the process *Customer Service by Design*.

Customer Service by Design is a process that illuminates the core conflicts that can arise out of each harmony's personality styles, thought processes and core motivations. When we understand what is important to each design, we can be more sensitive to the way each person processes information and how he or she will approach and avoid conflict. Once a person understands the do's and don'ts associated with each design harmony, that person is much better equipped to interact well with others.

Important values for the saturated harmony:

- Quality
- Professionalism
- Clearness
- Preciseness
- Timeliness
- Organization
- Appropriateness
- Respect for privacy
- Respect for personal space
- Appropriate humor
- Staying on track

A saturated person can be:

- Intimidating
- A perfectionist
- Aloof
- Demanding
- All business

Important values for the whitened design:

- Change
- Sociability
- Multitasking
- Fun
- Spontaneity

A whitened person can be:

- Annoying
- Indecisive
- Intrusive
- Inconsiderate

Important values for the grayed design:

- Thoroughness
- Sanitation
- Emotional availability
- Romance
- Experience
- Accountability
- Fiscal responsibility
- Consistency

A grayed person can be:

- Indecisive
- Inefficient
- Emotionally draining
- Slow moving/thinking

Important values for blackened design:

- Honest communication
- Realism
- Logic
- Emotional stability
- Compartmentalization
- Wit
- Credibility
- Resourcefulness

A blackened person can be:

- Overly logical
- Abrupt
- Insensitive
- Overbearing

Please note that not everyone will have all the can be's in his or her design, and some may not *be* that way as much as they *come across* that way. There's a difference. For example, saturated people who appear to be aloof may intimidate you, and you assume that they are thinking cold and cruel things. In reality, they are probably merely wondering what's for lunch.

ACHIEVING BALANCE

Certain designs have elements in common, but differences still exist even within these similarities. For example, the saturated design is authoritative in an introverted way. Saturated people are silent leaders. The blackened design is also authoritative, but in an extroverted way. Blackened people are verbal leaders. Both designs are autonomous, meaning that people who relate to both designs work well alone, and they have an independent focus, especially when it comes to achieving their goals. For example, politicians may benefit from driving their own agenda or platform. They are pushing what they believe. Keeping in perspective what needs to be done for a particular focus is an autonomous trait.

On the flip side, the grayed design is submissive in an introverted way; grayed people are silent followers. The whitened design, on the other hand, is also submissive, but in an extroverted way; whitened people are verbal (noncommittal) followers. Both designs are heteronymous.

Heteronymous is used to define a person who works well as part of a team. Heteronymous people are submissive in the sense that they are more concerned about the role of each team member and how everyone fits together. They have more of a sense of community or a collective conscience. For example, good project managers often hold heteronymous traits. They take more of a bottom-up approach than a top-down approach.

In Human Art theory, therefore, you have two prototype leaders (saturated and blackened) and two prototype followers (whitened and grayed). All designs are important, because together they achieve balance. A group working on a project would be very wise to include representatives from each design. They would all bring their strengths to the table, which would result in synergy. This kind of synergy must be how we were meant to operate in life, otherwise we would have all been created to look and act the same. Imagine, if you can, what *that* would be like! A committee made up entirely of people of the same design would be a disaster. Instead, as we understand our own design traits, we can use them to achieve harmony with the other three designs, enabling us to become interdependent with others and achieve a perfect balance.

CHAPTER 9

Human Art's Impact on
INTERPERSONAL RELATIONSHIPS

ONE OF THE MOST COMMON QUESTIONS PEOPLE ASK REGARDING THE HUMAN ART THEORY IS, "AM I A GOOD MATCH FOR MY SPOUSE/PARTNER/FRIEND?" THE ANSWER IS NOT WHETHER OR NOT YOU ARE A GOOD MATCH, BUT IN WHAT WAYS YOU ARE A GOOD MATCH. THE PROBLEMS WE ENCOUNTER WITH THOSE WHO ARE CLOSE TO US TYPICALLY ARISE BECAUSE OF THE NATURAL ATTRACTION AND CONFLICT INHERENT IN THE DIFFERENT DESIGNS AND PERSONALITY COLORS.

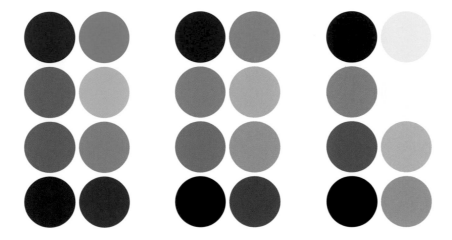

Opposite colors on the color wheel, when set side by side, can complement each other—but they can also clash. Think, for example, of red and green, blue and orange, or violet and yellow (or gold). You can take one of these colors and enhance it by putting its opposite next to it. A purple tablecloth, for instance, makes a striking display. However, it appears even more purple when you put a yellow flower up against it. The two colors enhance each other. The same principle applies to relationships; when put together, we enhance each other. The interesting phenomenon that occurs with human relationships is that while we are attracted to our opposites, the minute we deem them ours (*my* wife, *my* husband, *my* partner, *my* friend, etc.) we start the process of trying to change them and make them more like us. In essence, we chip away from them the very characteristics to which we were attracted. The very things we loved and admired about them are the same things that drive us nuts.

Within the harmonies, complementary traits *and* natural conflicts exist. The greatest aspect of that knowledge is that when we understand it, we can work with each other more productively. When confronted with a blackened person, for instance, you will no longer interpret their abruptness as rudeness, you will simply acknowledge that they speak the truth as they see it. Even better, you can start to actually *appreciate* what you may have found irritating before. In your mind you might think, "Look how blackened that person is! Isn't it great?" Or when whitened people are talking a lot, you will be able to simply acknowledge that they are being animated. Similarly, when a saturated person seems aloof, you will not think of him as cold—you will instead learn to appreciate his stillness. What has been a source of conflict can become an element of attraction.

SATURATED INTERACTIONS WITH OTHER SATURATED PEOPLE

Conflict

One of the most obvious conflict areas for saturated people is that they are clear thinkers and tend to hold their opinions as the gospel truth. They are very good at scanning a lot of information and picking out two or three important elements. Due to their central focus on preciseness and need for competence, they may lock in on their opinion or interpretation of the evidence and become very black and white in their presentation. In other words, saturated people may hold to their opinion in an uncompromising fashion and fail to consider the needs and opinions of those who disagree with their ideas—obviously a problem if two saturated people don't happen to have come to the same conclusions.

Attraction

When two saturated people get together they will have a lot in common, but their interaction won't really add the spice of something new. It's like having peas and peas for dinner. Of course, their secondary designs will often be different, so that is where the attraction will lie. If you put two saturated people together, you would end up with a lot of deep conversations, but there would probably not be a lot of attraction if they both were prototype saturated.

Saturated & Saturated

SATURATED INTERACTIONS WITH WHITENED PEOPLE

Conflict

From a saturated person's point of view, the whitened person may come across as silly and nonconforming to established rules and societal norms. In extreme cases, the saturated person may see the whitened person as irresponsible and unable to maintain a routine necessary to be successful. The saturated person may also be embarrassed by the whitened person's loud, busy and animated presentation. He or she may see the whitened person's lack of structure and nonconforming nature as inappropriate. The saturated person may also be threatened by the whitened person's spontaneous thought process and decision-making—thinking that the whitened person has not considered all the alternatives and consequences before taking a course of action.

Another basic conflict between the saturated and whitened design is that the saturated person is focused on precision and accuracy, while the whitened person may be difficult to pin down on any certain point. In fact, the whitened person may be noncommittal in many situations, frustrating the saturated need for preciseness. The saturated person also needs her personal space to be respected, and the whitened person does not always recognize this fact. Saturated and whitened people also experience the world differently. The whitened person is renewed and energized by social contact, but the saturated person would prefer to focus on the inner world of ideas, concepts and theories.

From the whitened person's perspective, the saturated person may seem stuffy and rule-bound. Because whitened people's focus is on social knowledge and experiencing all the fun that life has to offer, the saturated rigidity often makes them feel restricted and controlled. The whitened person may feel intimidated by the saturated person's imposed priorities. Due to the whitened person's social adeptness and desire to not hurt feelings, she may privately practice avoidance and become evasive in the face of control or dissatisfaction with the relationship.

Attraction

With regard to attraction, saturated people are drawn to whitened people because they are so cute and fun. Whitened people are willing to be free and spontaneous, and that is very attractive to those who don't come by those qualities naturally. It is as if whitened people give saturated people the permission to unstring their bow and relax for a minute. The saturated person is also periodically attracted to breaking out of his or her rigid structure and bending a few rules. A complementary connection also exists, because the saturated person is dominant and the whitened person is more submissive.

The whitened design is attracted to the saturated design because of a parental feeling in the relationship. The competence of the saturated person makes the whitened person feel secure. The whitened person will at times rely on the stability of the saturated person in terms of resource planning and direction. Once again, due to the whitened person being submissive and the saturated person being more dominant, a complementary connection forms.

Saturated

Grayed

SATURATED INTERACTIONS WITH GRAYED PEOPLE

Conflict

One of the major conflict areas between a saturated person and a grayed person is that the saturated person sees the grayed person as overly sensitive and idealistic. Also, in a saturated person's eyes, the grayed person is too detailed and tends to worry too much about insignificant things; whereas, the saturated person often loses credibility with the grayed person because he makes decisions too quickly and fails to consider all the contingencies. Because the saturated person quickly discerns the important elements of a situation and the grayed person studies all the details, the two may disagree on what is important in any given situation or what the timeline will be to address the problem. In other words, the saturated person is looking for precision and confirmation about her opinion in a decisive manner, while the grayed person is being indecisive and looking at and studying all the elements. In summary, the core conflict is that the saturated person is a clear thinker who likes to get to the point, and the grayed person wants to savor the details in a meticulous fashion and take the time to arrive at a meaningful conclusion. Another area of conflict appears to be that the grayed person is very romantic and idealistic, while the saturated person is a realist. Consequently, a grayed person's need for romance often is lost on the saturated counterpart, leading to resentment.

Attraction

In terms of attraction, saturated and grayed people get along well because they are both introverted. They are both good at considering ideas and established rules and are renewed by inner reflections. The saturated person can benefit from the grayed person's grasp of details and ability to point out the relationship between the elements which the saturated person may have missed or deemed unimportant. The saturated person can also gain insights from the grayed person when it comes to understanding situations which defy logic and beg for more intuition.

SATURATED INTERACTIONS WITH BLACKENED PEOPLE

Conflict

The saturated person may have conflict with the lack of refinement and sophistication of the blackened person, and the blackened person may find the saturated person pretentious. For example, the blackened person's practical, informal, hands-on approach to life may fly in the face of the saturated person's need for preparation, precision, discipline and sophistication. The blackened person just wants to get things done with no drama and in record time. Blackened people may appear to be careless, too rough or overly deliberate in their work or activities. When the saturated uncompromising trait meets the blackened overbearing trait, problems can arise and sparks can fly. The introverted strength of the saturated person and the extroverted strength of the blackened person leads to a power struggle.

Attraction

In terms of attraction, the saturated person likes to develop plans and strategies and then delegate important functions to the blackened person. Because a saturated person appreciates the blackened person's ability to get in and get things done, this partnership forms a complementary interaction. Saturated and blackened people are both autonomous and mutually respect independence and healthy separateness. Here again, however, the attraction would most likely be from the secondary design. Both designs produce chiefs, so it's not likely that they would attract through the dominant design or harmony.

Saturated
&
Blackened

WHITENED INTERACTION WITH OTHER WHITENED PEOPLE

Conflict

When two whitened people interact, they often compete for the attention in the room and strive to bring the focus to what they are doing or what excites them. Due to their high energy and spontaneous nature, they may tend to dominate conversation and often redirect the course of a discussion. Although two whitened partners both have this trait, they can each find it frustrating in the other person. Also, because they can be so animated and silly, they may appear to not care about standards of decorum, and may egg each other on, which can create trouble. Whitened people will also get blamed for flaking out on occasion due to their nonconforming, nonstructured nature. This problem occurs more frequently when nobody is around who wants to make the decisions.

Attraction

In terms of attraction, two whitened people will have a blast together because they appreciate each other's ability to break out and have fun. They will also be able to keep up with the high energy and spontaneous activity that is germane to the whitened design. They are both submissive, and will appreciate a noncontrolling quality in each other.

Whitened
Whitened

WHITENED INTERACTION WITH GRAYED PEOPLE

Conflict

In this relationship, the whitened person can appear scattered to the grayed person, while from the whitened person's perspective, the grayed person may come across as overly mature or too proper to be any fun. The two designs are often in pursuit of different results. The whitened partner makes quick decisions and bounces from one thing to another in a random order. The grayed person views that behavior as impulsive and irresponsible; he or she needs more time to think about things. The whitened person is weighed down by this grayed proclivity to worry and perform every activity in a meticulous, controlled fashion with attention to propriety. In other words, the grayed person is just too serious. A grayed person has difficulty with the non-conforming antics of the whitened person and may feel embarrassed by the whitened person's lack of regard for manners and etiquette. Therefore, a significant area of conflict arises when the whitened person tries to lighten up the grayed person or make him or her be more spontaneous or impulsive. Grayed people often feel overwhelmed with whitened people, because they move so fast and they have the ability to do so many things at once. The grayed person cannot relate to that. Contention can also arise because the whitened person is extroverted, energizing him or herself with social contact, while the grayed person is introverted, renewing him or herself with inner reflections. Since both are submissive, sometimes nobody is around to stir the pot.

Attraction

In terms of attraction, the whitened person is attracted to the nurturing nature of the grayed design. The grayed person can have a calming effect on the whitened high energy, and the whitened person can help the grayed person to have more fun. The two harmonies also relate in terms of being somewhat indecisive or noncommittal at times. Also, the whitened person's need to have fun and the grayed person's enjoyment of the process and the experience of life seem to form another complementary function.

Whitened & Blackened

WHITENED INTERACTION WITH BLACKENED PEOPLE

Conflict

When dealing with blackened people, the whitened person often feels restricted by the structure, guidelines and rules that govern tasks and getting the job done. The whitened person also may view the blackened person as too serious, or lacking fun and lightness. The blackened person's rugged nature may overwhelm the whitened person, as can the blackened person's forceful, direct manner and untiring focus on completing a task at the expense of having any fun. In this case, see the structured versus the nonstructured and the spontaneous versus task-oriented characteristics come into conflict.

The blackened person could see the whitened spontaneity as irresponsible and a hindrance to getting things accomplished. Being productive is not as important to a whitened person as it is to the blackened person. The two designs simply have different priorities. The whitened is more interested in the social aspects of any process, and the blackened is concerned about the bottom line.

Attraction

With regard to attraction, the whitened person is attracted to the informal, casual nature and strength of the blackened person. It's like putting a ladybug up against a lion. Once again, the blackened person may provide a sense of security for the whitened person, due to the dominant/submissive complement. While the whitened person is more inviting than the blackened person is, the whitened person can appreciate how approachable and warm blackened people can be. Blackened and whitened interaction is one of movement. They are both extroverted and fun. The whitened is slapstick silly, and the blackened has a dry wit. They are both the life of a party. They would therefore be able to have a great time together and enjoy the warmth and confidence they share. In summary, the complementary function is that the whitened design is the extroverted submissive and the blackened design is the extroverted leader, which promotes natural balance in the relationship.

GRAYED INTERACTION WITH OTHER GRAYED PEOPLE

Conflict

When two grayed people interact, chances for intuitive failures, lack of sensitivity or disagreements about appropriateness abound. Due to their introverted, intuitive, sensitive natures, grayed people often conceal worries and engage in complex scenarios of an interpersonal nature. Add a need to be proper and the grayed couple may have many conflicts because they don't express the complexity of their inner processes.

Attraction

Grayed people can also get along very well, because their interactions may result in a quintessential meeting of the minds. They can really get into their intricate thinking processes and relate to each other. They are often engaged in fine motor skills with their hands and they love reading. They love diagrams and patterns, so they can relate to each other in that way. They lend to each other rather than attract. Grayed people may find dramatic relief by sharing their worries with each other and comparing concerns.

Grayed *Blackened*

GRAYED INTERACTION WITH BLACKENED PEOPLE

Conflict

From the grayed perspective, the blackened person looks like the proverbial bull in a china shop. From the blackened perspective the grayed person may come across as a wimp. The blackened person's tough exterior and task-oriented approach to life often runs over the sensibilities of the grayed person. A grayed person is so sensitive, but the blackened design is so task-oriented that blackened people will often pass over the emotion of a situation in order to get things done. Both partners can end up frustrated in such a situation. This conflict is also seen in the grayed introversion, which is submissive, when brought up against the boldness of the blackened extroversion. The blackened design is up-front and direct, while the grayed person prefers to keep things inside and speak in euphemisms. So, when the grayed indecisiveness meets the blackened purposefulness, conflicts and misunderstandings arise that need to be resolved.

Attraction

In terms of attraction, the grayed design is drawn toward the strength and deliberateness of the blackened person. Grayed people appreciate the blackened ability to get things done. The grayed design can get overwhelmed in the details, so the blackened design complements that tendency by acting. The grayed person tends to be refined, and so the natural, rustic aspects of the blackened design are very attractive to the grayed person. (People are often attracted to qualities that they don't have.)

Along the same lines, the gentle quietude of the grayed person can be very calming, relaxing and balancing to the sometimes frantic pace of the blackened mindset. The blackened person may find what he or she is missing in the grayed person's gentleness and romantic tendencies.

BLACKENED INTERACTION WITH OTHER BLACKENED PEOPLE

Conflict

The conflict between two blackened people would be similar to the conflict between two large bulldozers trying to demolish the same small outhouse. Too much power can be counterproductive. Unless the two blackened people are able to agree on most, if not all, issues, their interactions will tend to be like two powerful rams locking horns.

Attraction

Two blackened people could build a village in one day. They are undeniably productive. They would appreciate each other's efficient qualities, and their warm, informal natures would complement each other. Also, their household would be virtually free of emotional drama, since they tend to value emotional stability. However, for two prototype blackened people, the attraction would most likely lie in having complementary secondary designs.

Let's look at a real-life example of a marriage where the partners both complemented and conflicted with one another. We worked with one couple, we'll call them Misty and Max, who were grayed and blackened, respectively. The grayed Misty wanted to plant flowers in the yard to make it look more romantic. The blackened Max didn't want to do it, because the cost for the flowers didn't fit into their budget. Max's mother decided to help by footing the bill and taking Misty to buy flowers for the yard. Very happy, Max went to work, and Misty and her kind mother-in-law went shopping. When Max came home from work, he drove up to the house, past a veritable symphony of flowers lining the driveway and yard, singing the glories of summer. As Max walked through the door, an excited Misty breathlessly asked, "Did you see what I did to the yard?" Bewildered, Max responded, "Did you mow the lawn?" Can you picture the argument that followed? The conflict here is that the blackened design sees the big picture and focuses on what still needs to be done. The grayed design sees the details along the way.

Misty accused Max of being insensitive, but that was not the case. As he was pulling up the driveway, he was focused on getting home to his wife. He was also thinking about paying all the bills and accomplishing his duties and chores, one of which was mowing the lawn. His focus was (and usually is) on the fundamentals. That quality is actually why Misty was initially attracted to him. Misty, on the other hand, focuses on the details. She takes the time to think things through and notices everything. Her romantic traits are what Max loved about her. After learning these facts about each partner, Max has learned to smell the flowers along the way, with Misty's help. Misty appreciates the fact that Max digs in and secures their home and relationship. Thus, they now work *with* each other's designs to defuse conflicts.

Opposites complete each other. Opposite colors, when mixed together, can have a neutralizing effect on each other. This neutralization can be a very powerful tool when it comes to the final effect of the color. Take orange and blue, for example. Orange by itself is a strong color. In some instances, it might be too loud. But suppose you were to mix in blue? If you add less blue than you have orange, the effect is a nice, toned down orange. The blue does not overtake it; rather, the blue softens it. The orange is softer and a little bit easier on the eye. It is neutralized slightly. If the blue tries to take over, however, then the orange is cancelled out, as well as the blue. So, too, in relationships we each get our chance to lead out. The other person should influence and strengthen us, rather than overwhelming us. Color can teach a very powerful lesson about working with each other. When you find and are attracted to your opposite, and you handle the relationship correctly, you will influence each other, rather than try to force each other to change. (You won't even *want* each other to change.) You become great helpmates. You will create an energy that continually draws you together.

Please understand that I have merely scratched the surface of some of the possible conflicts and attractions that can exist between the harmonies. The most important concept to take away from this discussion is that everyone is a combination of all four harmonies, and therefore the possibilities for attraction and conflict are countless. And isn't figuring out how to live together and appreciate each other what life is all about? Understanding others and conquering conflict could make a huge difference on this earth, and we *can* overcome conflict when we understand the dynamics of it. Knowledge truly is power. We all have the insight to understand, love and appreciate everyone with whom we come in contact. At some level, we can learn to appreciate each one of these designs and all the traits that go along with it. With that appreciation, conflict becomes less and less of an issue. Human Art, on the deepest level, is self-mastery and also mastering interpersonal relations and interactions—it is seeing all people in the eyes of the One who created them.

CHAPTER 10

Managing Inner DESIGN CONFLICTS

INTERPERSONAL RELATIONSHIPS ARE WITHOUT QUESTION CRUCIAL, BUT I WOULD ALSO LIKE TO ADDRESS ANOTHER OFTEN MORE PREVALENT KIND OF CONFLICT: THE CONFLICT WE FREQUENTLY FEEL WITHIN OURSELVES. I HAVE DESCRIBED AT GREAT LENGTH HOW UNDERSTANDING AND ACCEPTING OTHER PEOPLE'S DESIGNS IS SO IMPORTANT. NOW THE TRICK IS TO GET PEOPLE TO ACCEPT AND APPRECIATE THEIR OWN HARMONIES. I'M ALWAYS SORRY WHEN I HEAR PEOPLE GRUMBLING ABOUT THEIR DESIGN.

*O*ne time when I was in a store, I listened to a clerk (a very young and gorgeous girl) describing a pair of pants that she had tried on. She said that the pants made her legs look short and muscular; she was complaining about that description of herself. What she didn't understand was that she was beautiful, youthful and full of life, and that was exactly what her legs were communicating. She was animated, real and fun to talk to. In fact, she was absolutely darling, and her legs did nothing but tell the truth about her. She went on to say that she wished her legs were long and elegant. Those lines are also beautiful, but if *her* legs were long, she wouldn't be so animated and real. Her look—and this is true of us all—is how God sent her, and she was the kind of beautiful He wanted her to be.

Our bodies and personalities are a package deal, and they are all good. One of the most important things we can do for our own peace of mind and happiness is to believe in and *enjoy* who we are and what we look like.

At Human Art, we are often asked about whether plastic surgery is helpful to validate the self or rectify perceived flaws. Of course, we recognize that plastic surgery does have many important uses, but if you need or choose plastic surgery, please understand that it is crucially important to use the surgery to maintain your individual harmony, rather than change it. A wise surgeon who stays within the lines of the patient's harmony will always have a better result. For example, if the patient is animated and extroverted and opts for her nose to be changed to a line that communicates grace and elegance, then when people see that line in her nose, they expect her to act more elegant, refined and introverted. When the rules of harmony are not adhered to, the result can be contradiction and confusion. When a surgeon understands and complies with the principle of harmony within harmony, the result is congruent with the person's design and the bone structure continues to be what it was meant to be: a preview of the patient's inherent disposition.

*U*nfortunately, our inner conflict isn't restricted to the kind of dissatisfaction mentioned above. Even if (let's say *when*) we finally learn to love ourselves and our looks, we can still experience inner friction within our own designs. Of course, the dominant design always inherently leads out. But, just as the conflicts lie within the different designs from person to person, the same conflicts lie within an individual. These battles within ourselves are usually not as strong, because thankfully most people possess natural ways of balancing. A good example of opposing designs is a woman with whom we work in Human Art. She is saturated first and is very striking to the eye. When you see her she takes you aback in a chill of beauty that you rarely experience anywhere in nature. She is like the gleam of a silent lake with the moonlight reflecting on it. When you experience her for the first time, she tends to take your breath away. But there is a conflict in her design. One of her secondary designs is very warm and down to earth (blackened), so she has the desire to be warm and approachable. She is, in fact, both warm and approachable, once you get past her initial beauty. Her conflict lies in those two elements. When people stand back, in awe of her beauty, her secondary design immediately kicks in and she sees herself as not approachable or real, which is devastating to that part of her. She often misunderstands the breath that people take in awe of her as a bad thing. But her reaction is merely a result of her *own* perception—not other people's perceptions.

Every person, at some level, probably has a similar inner conflict. People are just not one-dimensional. My clients often express that they question themselves when this conflict surfaces. However, the realization that this inner disunity is perfectly natural should give them some peace of mind. Understanding how their designs tend to argue with each other helps them get past it.

Some people prefer a blackened rustic home while others prefer a refined grayed cottage. Just like in their design, blackened and grayed people often experience a conflict—they want elements of both. That conflict is okay as it communicates who they are.

*A*nother person who works with us provides an additional example of competing designs. She is blackened and grayed. As is often the case, she has almost an equal degree of each element, proportionally, within her design. This person speaks and communicates very directly, but she will then go home and worry about how she came across. Both her directness and her sensibility about it are two important factors within each design. The fact that these elements of her personality make her question herself is perfectly natural. Understanding this phenomenon is a good place to start in coping with it. Our competing inner voices are no longer a problem as long as we understand how they work within our design.

CHAPTER II

Personality &
PERSONALITY COLORS

ANOTHER LEVEL OF HUMAN ART IS PERSONALITY COLORS. ONCE WE HAVE PULLED A COLOR FAN TO ESTABLISH A CLIENT'S DESIGN, WE THEN PULL A SEPARATE COLOR FAN USING ALL THE COLORS ON HER COLOR WHEEL. BY HOLDING THE COLORS UP TO HER, WE ESTABLISH THE BEST OF EACH COLOR AND PUT THEM IN ORDER OF HER BEST PROJECTING COLORS. WE THEN INTERPRET THESE COLORS BY WHAT WE CALL THE TRUE INTENT OF THE COLOR OR COLOR PERSONALITY PROFILING. THIS PROCESS TELLS US ON A DEEPER LEVEL, SECONDARY TO HER DESIGN, HOW SHE INTERACTS AND RELATES TO PEOPLE.

For example, one of the men on our staff (we'll call him Wally) has a very serious design. He relates to the saturated and grayed harmonies, which makes him very serious and wise. The interesting thing about his design is that his first personality color is yellow. The yellow is saturated and grayed, so it is still true to his inherent qualities, but it sometimes makes him break out into playfulness, which is what yellow communicates. He has the need to be liberated when things get too regimented. He is very serious about what he does, but is always the one playing jokes, and just when you least expect it he is acting very juvenile and fun.

Human Art has so many dimensions! In all the years Human Art has been analyzing individuals, we always come up with the same conclusion: each person is one of a kind.

Some examples of personality colors and the way a person interacts and relates to other people are:

Blue

- Introverted
- Cool emotions and feelings
- Intangible
- Alert to distinctions
- Serious
- Spiritually (not referring to religion) quiet
- Loves change, progress, the unknown

Black

- High quality
- Serious
- Somber
- Authoritative
- Intimidating
- Precise
- Sophisticated
- Visually dominant

Green

- Logical
- Compassionate
- Balanced/harmonious
- Self-respecting
- Organized
- Nurturing
- Efficient
- Trustworthy

Violet

- Merciful
- Just
- Dignified
- Noble
- Proud
- Compassionate

White

- Authoritative (in a softer, more open way than black)
- Light
- Bright
- Clean
- Spiritual
- Credible

Gray

- Serene
- Private
- Subtle
- Dreamy
- Expensive
- Idealistic
- Indecisive
- Matte
- Limp

Red

- Yang
- Autonomous
- Large muscle dominant
- Active
- Masterful
- Excited
- Impulsive
- Good leader

Fuchsia

- Outwardly expressive of peace
- Calming
- Stimulating
- Visually exciting in its intensive form
- Soft
- Independent

Pink

- Pampered
- Warm
- Small muscle dominant
- Low endurance
- Hesitant
- Sensual
- Follower
- Soft
- Pulls back

Yellow

- Lively
- Easy
- Radiant
- Stimulating
- Liberated
- Spontaneous
- Optimistic
- Zestful

Orange

- Considerate
- Uninhibited
- Reasonable
- Persuasive
- Rhythmic
- Energetic
- Victorious

Peach (Baby Orange)

- Light
- Warm
- Sensuous
- Sexy
- Charming
- Dependent
- Delicate
- Subliminal leader

Brown

- Wise
- Secure
- Broad spectrum
- Protective
- Sturdy
- Grounded
- Stalwart
- Rich
- Strong

Gold

- Practical
- Rule-follower
- Service-oriented
- Parental
- Hardworking
- Prepared
- Traditional
- Leader

There is a version of color for every person for each harmony.

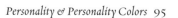

Understanding that each color has its positive and negative side is also important. We call the negative side the "can be's." The can be's are a very important part of the designs. Over the years we have found that in each particular design certain tendencies exist if the person with that design is feeling at all insecure or acting in an unhealthy manner. For example, if a whitened person is trying too hard to prove himself, he could be obnoxious. If a saturated person is trying too hard to prove herself, she could be perceived as condescending. A blackened person could be too blunt and hurt feelings. A grayed person could worry too much or become incommunicative. To be aware of the can be's and try to avoid them is healthy.

We have also found over the years that each personality color has its correlating can be's. People who react negatively seem to do so in the same manner as others who relate to that same color. For example, green people often react with strong emotion when their stability is threatened. Now, not all green people have the entire list of can be's. We have found that if green people do react negatively, their reaction tends to be in the list of green can be's. The same holds true for all the other colors. The can be's are easily dealt with—often when the individuals are exposed to the color itself. We have observed that surrounding people with a personality color often helps promote the positive traits of their design. This interesting observation implies that color is therapeutic and teaches us how important our colors are.

The lightness or darkness of a color is also critical to the personality colors. If the color is light, then people tend to have a lighter version of that color's characteristics. If the color is deeper, then people tend to have more serious traits that relate to the color. For example, if people relate to green in their harmonies, they like order and structure. If their personality color is deep green, their version of structure might be so regimented that it becomes traditional. If their personality color is a light green, they would crave order but might not have the follow-through to achieve or maintain it. (In that case, for their sanity, I would suggest a housekeeper.)

Let's review this process. So far, we establish the design for an individual by pulling her colors and finding the amount of each harmony. We then find her correlating lines, sound and movement that establishes her unique attractiveness, movement and thinking. We then move on to her personality fan, which shows us more accurately how she interacts and relates to others.

Clearly, Human Art is a very specific science. We are proud of that fact. Putting each person in a dimension occupied by no one else, ever, is exciting. Every person is unique, and we have found a way to measure that uniqueness.

Chinese Philosophy:
YIN & YANG

IN A FEW PLACES IN THIS BOOK, THE WORDS YIN AND YANG HAVE POPPED UP. THESE WORDS, BORROWED FROM THE CHINESE, ARE MOST APPROPRIATE WHEN USED TO DESCRIBE THE QUALITIES OF BODY AND FACIAL DESIGN.

Thousands of years ago, Chinese philosophers wrote their ideas about how to define things that differ versus things that are the same. These philosophers realized that any quality can be described only in relationship to its opposite. We perceive hot only in contrast to cold, dry to wet, light to dark, hard to soft, etc. This law of opposition, or duality, they said, could be observed in everything. The world is, at its most basic, divided into day and night, men and women, movement and stillness. The philosophers ascribed the word yang to things that move and are warm, firm, bold, bright, large, angular and open. Yin, they reserved for things that are still, cold, yielding, reserved, shadowy, small, rounded and mysterious. Although the two words implied opposition, yang could never be found without some yin and yin without some yang; that is, all things are in some proportion a combination of both. To the Chinese, the countless different combinations of yin-ness and yang-ness made all things unique. The interesting fact about yin and yang is that we all possess both qualities. The yin and the yang in each of us contrast with each other, or point each other out.

YIN & YANG ANALYSIS

	YIN	YANG
BODY STRUCTURE	Feminine, small features, small bones, refined, dainty, fragile, rounded, petite, elongated	Angular, broad shoulders, tall, sturdy, athletic, stately, large, clear cut, erect
APPEARANCE & MOVEMENT	Graceful, impulsive, romantic, languid, understated, subtle, methodical, feminine, youthful, delicate, light, quick, natural, fresh	Dynamic, energetic, vital, bold, dramatic, sensuous, earthy, vigorous, firm, sophisticated, dramatic, high fashion
COLORING	Marked clarity of skin, usually fair, low contrast value, cool skin tones (often blue undertones), delicate, smooth	Warm skin tones, olive undertones, high contrast value, darker hair tending to be chestnut, red or golden
FACIAL STRUCTURE	Overall roundness to shape of face, rounded cheeks, small dimples, elongation of oval face, few marked facial planes	Angular facial planes, square jaw, angular cheek bones, oval face shape, sharp profile, delicately chiseled features
EYES	Rounded, wide open, no eyebrow peak, oval eyes, oval eyebrows, delicate eyebrows	Large, oval eyes; peaked, evenly arched or heavy eyebrows
NOSE	Delicate, short, turned up, straight, refined	Long, straight, sharply chiseled, angled, large, flared nostrils
MOUTH	Rounded, bow-like, small, oval, "S" lined curves	Full, peaked upper lip, even and oval
ATTITUDE	Dependent, gentle, tactful, receptive, quick, intuitive, natural, simple, naïve	Self-sufficient, aggressive, decisive, reserved, dominating, analytical, sophisticated, air of experience, ability to disguise or dramatize feelings

Perhaps, one of the most concrete examples of Yin/Yang is the elephant. When you look at an elephant, the Yang is obvious with its size, strength and boldness. But the yin can be seen in its tail, voice and the end of its trunk/snout.

How to Use the Assessment Instrument &
DIAGNOSTIC PROCESS

THE PERSONAL DESIGN ASSESSMENT PROFILE IS AN INSTRUMENT THAT AIDS IN DIAGNOSING A CLIENT. THE HARMONIES RUN DOWN THE LEFT SIDE AND THE DESIGN ELEMENTS RUN ACROSS THE TOP. THE PERSON CONDUCTING THE ASSESSMENT MERELY CIRCLES THE ELEMENTS HE OR SHE OBSERVES FROM LEFT TO RIGHT AND FROM TOP TO BOTTOM, STARTING WITH THE SATURATED HARMONY AND WORKING DOWN TOWARD THE BLACKENED HARMONY. THE DESIGN PROFILE STARTS TO TAKE FORM AFTER THE ASSESSOR HAS INTERACTED WITH THE SUBJECT FOR JUST A FEW MINUTES. AS THE ASSESSOR STARTS TO CIRCLE THE OBSERVABLE DESIGN ELEMENTS, THE PRIMARY DESIGN HARMONY BECOMES EVIDENT. BY TAKING THE TIME TO COMPLETE THE ENTIRE ASSESSMENT, ONE CAN START TO ORDER THE DESIGNS BY COUNTING ACROSS THE PROFILE FROM LEFT TO RIGHT. IN OTHER WORDS, THE ASSESSMENT RESULTS WILL UNVEIL THE INDIVIDUAL'S UNIQUE PROFILE, MEASURING EACH ELEMENT AND THE CLIENT'S DEGREE OF ENDORSEMENT.

One of our clients displays repeating oval lines in her bone structure. Her visual features are striking, sculptured, regal and polished. Her contrast value is medium to high. Her personality style is sometimes introverted, competent, intimidating and precise. Her sound is authoritative and stately, and she is still, controlled and precise in her movement. Also, she has some warmth in her skin tones and personality, and she is strong and rustic. She is a compartmentalized thinker and at times task-oriented. She has a strong voice and deliberate movement. She also has a hint of youthfulness. After reviewing the assessment, we find that her primary design is saturated. Her secondary design is blackened and she has a small amount of whitened.

Human Art measures each person's design based on 13 design elements and a host of personality colors. The process starts with a comprehensive color reading, which goes through 400 colors (saturated, tints, shades and tones).

Discovering the best projecting and neutral colors helps us create the person's color fan. We then go through the chosen colors and select which are the best of the projecting and neutral fans. The color reading is the most accurate assessment in arriving at the various levels of saturation, whitened, grayed and blackened design because the color can be mathematically arranged to know how much white, gray or black is added to a person's color wheel.

During the color reading, the colorist starts to develop a hypothesis based on the observation of the lines, sound and movement noticed during the initial contact with the client. To deepen the analysis, the colorist starts to observe contrast value, scale, yin/yang, visual features and texture. Thus far in the process, the colorist is starting to see a pattern emerge in terms of the predominant design and the second and third harmonies. In other words, the elements are starting to cluster in a way that supports the initial hypothesis.

Once the practitioner completes the initial color reading and observes and documents the primary design elements, he or she continues to finalize the assessment through ongoing interactions, by examining personality style, thought process, can be's and the client's central focus. Over time the profile is refined until the practitioner and client arrive at a unique design profile that rings true to and validates the client's knowledge of her inherent qualities. Once the client understands the design profile, she feels more permitted to be herself. This leads to ongoing growth and personal development.

THE PERSONAL DESIGN ASSESSMENT PROFILE & DECISION TREE

	COLOR	LINE	CONTRAST VALUE	VISUAL FEATURES	PERSONALITY STYLE	THOUGHT PROCESS
SATURATED	Pure chroma Color Cool coloring	Ovals Parallel lines Fast diagonal	High	Striking Sculptured Dramatic Serious Regal Polished	Introvert Competent Sophisticated Intimidating Disciplined Influential Prepared Precise	Left brained Logical Decisive Clear thinker
WHITENED	Tints Warm coloring	Circles Part of circles Repetition	Medium	Youthful Animated Cheerful Inviting	Extraverted Spontaneous High energy Silly Childlike Social	Nonstructured Nonconforming Unassuming Spontaneous Trusting
GRAYED	Tones Cool coloring	Elongated "S" curves	Low to medium	Elegant Dignified Mysterious Delicate Refined Soft	Introverted Proper Meticulous Negotiable	Intuitive Complex Idealistic Sensitive Worrier

BLACKENED	Shades
	Warm coloring
		Angular
		Vertical lines
		  forming right
		  angles
		Geometric
			Medium to high	Rustic
				Bold
				Large muscle
				Strong
				Earthy
				Rugged
				Tough
					Extraverted
					Direct
					Practical
					Structured
					Informal
					Initiative
					Assertive
						Compartmentalize
						  information
						Task oriented

The Personal Design Assessment
Profile is an instrument that aids
in diagnosing a client.

SOUND	MOVEMENT	SCALE	TEXTURE	YIN/YANG	CAN BE	CENTRAL FOCUS
Authoritative Articulate Stately	Still Minimal movement Controlled Sleek Precise	Large features	Smooth Stiff Shiny	Yang	Uncompromising	Precise Competent
Constant rapid speech Giggling	Bouncing Busy Animated Maximum amount of movement	Small features	Soft Crisp Lightweight Decorated	Yin	Noncommittal	Social Have fun
Eloquent Reserved Minimal Small voice	Graceful Flowing Languid	Small to medium features Medium to large features	Soft Limp Billowy Sheer Matte	Yin	Indecisive	Know details Enjoy process/experience
Loud Raspy Rough	Deliberate On purpose Medium	Large features	Rough Nubby Thick Matte Dull	Yang	Overbearing	Get the job done

CHAPTER 14
Mood, Color &
SCENT

ONE OF THE MOST POWERFUL MANIFESTATIONS OF COLOR IS A COLOR EXPERIENCE, OR THE WAY WE EXPERIENCE COLOR WHEN WE SEE IT OR ARE SURROUNDED BY IT. HUMAN ART TEACHES THAT WE CAN HAVE A COLOR EXPERIENCE WHEN WE SMELL A COLOR AS WELL. NOW, I CAN SENSE THE RAISED EYEBROWS THAT THE LAST SENTENCE CAUSED. HOW ON EARTH, I HEAR YOU ASK, DO YOU SMELL A COLOR? WELL, HOW DO YOU FEEL WHEN YOU PEEL A DELICIOUS ORANGE AND SMELL ITS SCENT? HOW ABOUT WHEN YOU WALK OUTSIDE ON A MOUNTAIN ROAD? THE GREENERY AROUND YOU HAS A CERTAIN GROUNDING, YET NURTURING SMELL. YOU FEEL REFRESHED. I'M ALWAYS AMAZED AT HOW I CAN RUN OR RIDE A BIKE IN THE MOUNTAINS FOR HOURS, YET THE SAME DISTANCE IN THE CITY SEEMS IMPOSSIBLE. SOME OF THIS PHENOMENON CAN BE EXPLAINED BY THE HEALING SENSATION THE COLOR GREEN INSPIRES IN BOTH SIGHT AND SMELL. THAT IS A COLOR EXPERIENCE AND IT HAPPENS TO US ALL EVERY DAY. IN FACT, SMELLING A SCENT THAT HAS A CORRELATING COLOR IS THE FASTEST WAY TO HAVE A COLOR EXPERIENCE.

*T*he following story beautifully illustrates my point. Some time ago, I met an instructor in a school where the morale was quite low. The grades were average at best. She described the colors in the school as subdued and gray. The borders were dark and dreary. The teachers and administration soon realized that the colors were not desirable for a classroom atmosphere. So they painted the classrooms with an array of beautiful colors, such as subdued orange and little bits of red. Soon, the administration started seeing a marked difference in students' attitudes. The morale was lifting, and most importantly, grades were coming up. Are you ready for the clincher? This particular school was a school for the blind. True story. Somehow those students, through their other senses (including olfactory) were aware of the colors without actually seeing them.

We simply don't realize how much color affects us, yet we use color experiences to keep order in our society. When we see an orchestra, for instance, the musicians are all dressed in black. This color is authoritative and demands respect. It has a certain finality to it—it's the last word. That's why a priest often wears black. On the other hand, we wrap a newborn baby in soft pink or blue. Pink, which softens and gives a sense of pampering, usually surrounds baby girls. You automatically start pampering the child. Now, picture an orchestra all in pink. What a different picture! And on the flip side, we would never hand a mother her newborn baby girl wrapped in black. These are all color experiences we have, and they can go so much deeper than just sight.

At our laboratory in Green Valley, Utah, we mix essential oils for each of the seven colors needed to have a color experience. Each oil has its own smell that matches the path of its correlating color. Violet, for example, comes from the essential oils of African violets, as well of other natural essential oils that go along with the color path of violet. When a client smells the oils, she simply indicates whether the scent is a yes, a no, or a maybe. If a particular scent smells good to a client, that is the color experience she needs. A craving for a particular scent means that is the deficient color in her life. If the client rejects a scent, she is sufficiently balanced in that color.

When a client smells the oils, she simply indicates whether the scent is a yes, a no, or a maybe.

The same experience occurs naturally in our lives, as well. When we smell a fresh-cut orange we experience all that comes with the color orange. When we smell a green tree or the green grass, we experience the nurturing yet stabilizing effect of green. We reap the same benefit if we see a green color on a piece of paper, walk into a green room, or smell the essential oils from an evergreen tree. When you recognize what color or colors you need, you can then recognize your daily moods. The right smells will help lighten your load or help balance you. When you smell the scents of the colors or see the colors, you can recognize where you are in terms of emotions or logic. We call these our moods.

At Human Art, we call the right scents "mood elevators." A mood changes the way we think and feel. If you're still not convinced, then take into account the fact that the 2004 Nobel Prize was awarded to two scientists, Axel and Buck, for their research into the importance of the olfactory system—the sense of smell. They discovered that more of our human genetic structure is attributed to smell than to any other sense, except for the immune system. No wonder scent has such a profound effect on our color experience when we smell and breathe in these colored oils.

As we breathe in negative and positive molecules in the air, they discharge certain olfactory receptors in the nose, firing electrical impulses through our limbic system—the seat of our emotions. Thus, our sense of smell profoundly affects the emotional quality of our lives. Human Art has been able to tap into this very system to enhance the color experience.

*F*or example, years ago we had a new employee. She went to buy some lunch a few doors down, and she came back with a green, licorice-type candy, Sprite (green can) and spearmint gum (green package). Not the most healthful lunch, granted, but I could immediately see that she was most likely craving green. Sure enough, when I described to her what green was about, she stated that those qualities were exactly what she was missing in her life. We have this type of experience over and over.

Carole Coombs writes,

Everyone has an inherent frequency pattern—like a harmonic chord, a palate of colors, a signature or a voiceprint. This imprint is carried in the nucleus of every cell and forms our natural tendencies, our body design, and even our personality traits. We could call this pattern our original understructure [our harmony.]

But as we move through life's many challenges, we experience differing levels of human endeavor—such as thinking, acting , feeling and even creating.

All these endeavors that Carole Coombs lists, (thinking, acting, feeling and creating) are actions that correlate with the *mood* that a particular person is in at a particular time.

So, scents have everything to do with recognizing your daily mood through color. Scent is the fastest way to recognize what emotional balance you need for a given time in your life. Therefore, when we have established your design, or harmony, and we have determined in which of the four logics you function, we can balance you emotionally through color. Does that seem far-fetched? It is a fact that when we have a certain emotion, our bodies create a chemical. When we are off balance in our emotions, we need different emotions to achieve that balance. When you smell the scent of the correlating color, you simply release those feelings. We have found that if you need the scents that are carefully mixed to match the frequency of each color, you also crave to see and otherwise experience the color of that same frequency. Carole Coombs follows her earlier statement about our own imprint as follows:

Like sound, color and touch, scent is actually a wave pattern—a frequency. As we breathe in, it passes over the olfactory receptors, where it is differentiated and transferred to the limbic system, the seat of our emotions and moods.

Our moods even move through color. Yes, we can even measure, and more importantly, balance our moods through color.

Like strings of a guitar that resonate with a certain harmonic quality, our own imprint is distinct, and yet, as we move over those strings in cadences soft and sweet, deep and low, or maybe high and quick, our heart follows, changing our mood and physiology along with the melody.

Our aromatic essential oils and smelling salts are not perfumes, but a blend of natural volatile essences selected from the finest available. Each individual essence was chosen for its particular effect on the senses. In combination, they interact to enliven and clarify the primary levels of human nature—physical, emotional and mental.

The following is Carole Coombs' definition of each color mood.
The color or colors we choose determine our best functioning state.

Red: The melody of red says, "Stop thinking about it and just do it!" If you are in the mood to express your adventurous nature, be red. This frequency pattern stimulates glandular secretions that the senses report as delight, bringing excitation at the cellular level and heightened activity to body parts and passions. Red promotes physical activity, aliveness and free movement through life's difficult changes. It enlivens the senses and turns the heart toward magical moments of affection and delight.

Blue: The rhythm of blue is an antidote for the "blues." Blue promotes introspection and resolution. When you are blue, you remove yourself from the crowd to uncover your innermost feelings and beliefs. To be blue is to look to yourself for solutions, to discover those things that truly bring you satisfaction and delight, to find your own path. In times of discouragement, trial, loss and regret, this mode moves through the shadows within, resolves feelings of injustice and unworthiness, and brings tranquility and inner strength.

Yellow: The light and cheerful voice of yellow is like early dawn when all that we have pondered over and reminisced about—the shadowy forms of night—are suddenly released and chased away by the light of a new day. You simply let go and move on as you awaken to the glory and wonder that is present in this bright, new world. Yellow makes you feel as if an invitation is offered to partake of life's moveable feast and participate in new possibilities you may not have seen before. Yellow promotes developing new skills, joining the crowd, lightening up and living joyously.

Indigo: Are you ready to realize your vision? If so, your mood is deep indigo. This frequency leads you into a state where clutter in the mind disappears, concentration is focused, nonessentials are eliminated and ideas become clear. Whether you want to undertake a new beauty regimen, redo your house, participate in social reform, write a book, compose a concerto, develop new scientific insight and know-how, or bring relief to the world's suffering people, this mode is where visions and dreams become real.

— Carole Coombs

We can see that we move in and out of each color at different times of our lives. Wouldn't it be great if we all could understand our inherent designs, then move on to understanding our personalities, and finally our moods? I know many men out there who would pay a lot of money to understand their wives' moods, and vice versa. We can all come a lot closer to understanding each others' moods if we can understand our own. Understanding goes a long way toward tolerance.

If you think this kind of understanding and tolerance is impossible, I'm happy to tell you you're wrong. At the Green Valley Spa, this mood education has been happening for years. First, we promote the understanding of the design, then the careful detection of the person's mood. Then we mix a simple oil and *voila!* Understanding takes place.

Of course, moods are tied directly into emotions. When you simply surround yourself with the scent that appeals to you, the emotions that go with it will be what you need for that time. As we all know, these needs can change daily. The best way to know what color and matching scent you need is to recognize that if you need it, you crave it. The best way to achieve balance is to surround yourself with the color or colors you find yourself craving.

Human Art is so encompassing! It can give you a powerfully understanding of not only how you were put together and how you interact with others, but also of such intangible things as what mood you are passing through at any given time, and if necessary, what to do about it.

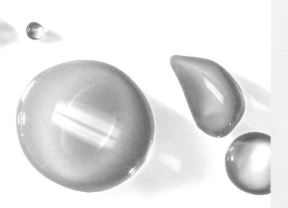

To my surprise, I have had many clients over the years who have smelled the scented oils with their correlating colors and burst into tears in a release of joyful emotion. They then describe how much better they feel. These reactions can happen naturally, as well, when a person sees and smells what he or she needs. For instance, I know of a particular woman who leads a wonderful, very structured and accomplished life. She balances a time-sensitive career with a family, and she is very involved in her church and the community. She is able to do all this because her design is very structured, and she has the ability to compartmentalize and organize. As I described the adjectives of blue to her one day, she found herself getting swept away to a place she craves—the ocean. She hungers for the intangible freedom of the sea and the sky, and absolutely loves to go to any beach. She knew what she lacked, and it was blue. Blue is what she craved (and needed) for balance.

In contrast, I know another woman whose life is creative and less structured. The nature of her career is very spontaneous, and she has to balance many things in no particular order. She had an exaggerated reaction to the green oil. She could not stop smelling it. It made her feel grounded, like she was lying in the grass. I loved watching her response. Even though I understand how it happens, I am still constantly amazed at how a simple scent can turn a day around!

CHAPTER 15
The Complete PICTURE

THE RENOWNED POET, MAYA ANGELOU, TELLS A BEAUTIFUL STORY ABOUT HER RELATIONSHIP WITH HER MOTHER. WHEN MAYA WAS YOUNG SHE VISITED HER MOTHER. WHEN IT WAS TIME TO GO, HER MOTHER WALKED HER DOWN THE HILL. AT THE BOTTOM OF THE HILL, SHE TURNED AND SAID, "MAYA, I THINK YOU ARE THE GREATEST WOMEN I HAVE EVER MET." MAYA SAYS THAT SHE THEN THOUGHT TO HERSELF, "MAYBE I WILL DO SOMETHING GREAT." MAYA'S MOTHER SAW THE MASTERPIECE IN MAYA AND ESSENTIALLY GAVE HER THE PERMISSION TO FIND HER GREATNESS. MAYA ANGELOU INTERNALIZED HER MOTHER'S WORDS. SHE TOOK A LOOK AT HERSELF AND ACCEPTED WHAT HER MOTHER SAID ABOUT HER AS TRUE. LIKE MAYA'S MOTHER, I SEE THE MASTERPIECE IN EVERY PERSON I ENCOUNTER. I SEE IT IN YOU AND I GIVE YOU PERMISSION TO BE GREAT.

I believe that those people who tell themselves daily about the good in their design are the ones with esteem, contrasting with those who choose to compare themselves against someone who is not like them at all. It's like a ballerina being frustrated that she cannot be a cheerleader. Instead of being the best ballerina she can be and loving that about herself, she focuses on the fact that she cannot cheer and feels disappointed and stuck her whole life. What a waste! She could instead be a beautiful ballerina and celebrate what a good cheerleader her neighbor might be. We all win when we stay true to who we really are.

Human Art adds a new dimension to expression and harmony because it does not apply beauty to any one individual as if it were a hat that we could plop down on our heads and then say, "There, *now* you are beautiful!" Human Art recognizes the attractiveness within each harmony and what it communicates, down to the smallest detail. It then gives you direction, teaches you how to magnify your innate strengths and enables you to better interact with others. It validates you and gives you permission to be who you are, which is very empowering. Human Art is not so much a state of mind as it is the reality and realization of your greatness. Sometimes you simply forget to see that greatness for what it is, instead of for what it's not.

It's time to see the uniqueness in each and every person and appreciate each communication for what it was intended to be. I love people who are refined. I also love people who are animated, sophisticated or down-to-earth. I try to see every individual through the eyes of the One who made him or her with precise intention. A work of art, when finished, is most exciting to the master who painted it. Why? Because he saw every line, every stroke, before it was even on canvas, and he knows the intention of the work. When the masterpiece all comes together, the artist anticipates the communication his opus will convey to others. He looks forward to the emotional reaction others will have to it.

Understanding and valuing the different communications becomes so easy! You just need to look, and more importantly, *know* what you are looking for. Start looking. Look at every person around you. What is his communication? What does she say and how does she say it? If you apply the Human Art principles, you will not only look, you will really *see*.

When you start recognizing and applying the Human Art elements, you also can see yourself in a clearer light. As you watch yourself in day-to-day life, or even when you see yourself in pictures, you can carefully measure the masterpiece that you are. The smallest line in your features communicates volumes to the world about who you are and why you act and think the way you do. That line reveals what you like and dislike and how you are comfortable being treated. It tells you about the hairstyles and clothes in which you look your best. Some force greater than us made you, and made you for specific reasons. You were intended to conquer things that only you can conquer, and in a way only you can conquer them. No one else is like you. Find yourself. Celebrate yourself. Strengthen yourself. Be yourself!

*L*et me tell you about Francy, a woman that was introduced to Human Art years ago. Francy was a great presenter. She took a course in public speaking and was actually encouraged by a leader to present in a certain way and *not* be herself. Fortunately for her and all those who listen to her speak, she believed in her *own* style of greatness and made the conscious decision to go onstage and be who she was. She chose to use the strengths that came from her inherent qualities, and to her surprise, she got a standing ovation. That was not the last standing ovation she got. Francy is a great leader, with skills that her peers acknowledge because she leads in an innate way that's appropriate for her. Many people ask her how she achieves this type of success. That's easy. She does it by just being her.

A Penny and a Pen

In this book, I have mentioned your *imprint* several times. Your imprint is the effect that you and your design have on people around you. You leave it wherever you go. It could be that the way you talk and move lights up someone's day whenever you are around him or her. You never know the effect, or imprint, you might have on people, so you should never underestimate your own worth to them. We are all important to somebody—usually many somebodies. Let the number one somebody you are important to be yourself.

anny was 23 years old. I don't know why, but he could not truly believe in or see his greatness, even though he knew all about the different designs, including his own. He had a great understanding of Human Art, and used it in his daily practice as a stylist. He changed many people's lives. For some reason, however, he just could not internalize his own worth. These feelings are not unusual; many times we can value others, but when it comes to ourselves we have a harder time.

One February day a few years ago, I was with Danny, and we were talking and laughing like we often did. He did a small favor for me and in a joking spirit he asked to be compensated for it. In the same spirit, I searched for something with the least amount of monetary value I could possibly find. I came upon a free pen and a penny in my purse. Thinking I was so clever, I handed the worthless items to him. He laughed and then expressed how much I meant to him.

A few hours after I had left him, I got a phone call and was informed that Danny had put action to his feeling of being unvalued and was gone. He had taken his own life. I immediately went to his home and ran into his room. There on his nightstand I found three things that were of value to him: his scriptures, the penny and the pen. In an instant, the penny and the pen's value went from worthless to priceless. Why? Because those simple items represented interactions and relationships I had with him. They were part of that last interaction: the laughing, the way he made me feel around him...his imprint.

You have an imprint. Believe me, no one else has it. It simply cannot be replaced. Danny cannot be replaced. If nothing else, know that if you have a hard time believing in your own imprint, somebody else does. You can internalize that fact alone. You were not randomly made. You were carefully put together, for a reason. That reason may not even so much be for yourself alone, but for how you affect others in relationships around you.

Please walk away from this book understanding you were formed like a wonderful sculpture. Your lines may be soft and refined or bold and energetic. Every line, every bone, means something. Find esteem in the fact that you are not an accident. You are a masterpiece—and so is the person standing next to you.

In a powerful Greek myth, 12 Greek gods were on a mission to send humans to earth to find their worth. The 12 were assigned the task of making the humans' worth difficult to find. The gods feared that if humans discovered their worth too easily, they wouldn't appreciate it once they had found it. So the 12 set off to plan this task. The first of the 12 said, "Let's hide their worth high in the mountaintops. It will be difficult to find there." The other 11 gods disagreed, and stated that the humans were so eager for their greatness that they would climb the mountain in a day a find it. The second of the 12 said, "Let's bury it deep in the sea. That will truly make it difficult for them to find." Once again, the others disagreed. They feared that the humans' eagerness to discover their greatness would lead them to dive into the sea and find it very quickly. Then the wise Greek god who was over the other 12 came down and offered a solution. He said, "Simply hide each human's greatness inside of him; he will never look there."

When I heard this myth years ago, how true it rang. So, now that nearly all is said and done, I urge you to look inside yourself—not with a blank stare, but with new eyes and the tools that we have given you to specifically find yourself and what you are about. Where have you left your imprint? Where does it still need to be experienced? How do you now define your uniqueness? What are you here on this earth to do? You're not finished, because you're still here. You hold the strengths and abilities to do what is intended for you, inside of you. What is left to overcome, accomplish, endure or invent? Do it!

You are an equation that relates to color. Your lines communicate a brilliance seen nowhere else. You are a harmony that works in its own path, through its own frequency. Start down that path and vow not to get sidetracked by trying to be something you are not. You're better than that! Travel the road that is your intended path. Admire others for their journey and the strengths they have to accomplish it.

You are an individual with your own communication. Just like that fine art displayed in a museum, you stand alone—a wonderful, masterful, delightful, *beautiful* piece of Human Art.

Armed with knowledge of your inherent nature,
the truth will set you free.
Run back to the imprint you were meant to be.

BROOK & ROD THORNLEY

The driving force behind Human Art, Brook Thornley is an author, award-winning cosmetologist and Master Educator for Matrix, a division of L'Oréal. For over 25 years Brook has worked in the family's salon and day spa, helping with the development of Human Art Design. Together with her husband, Rod Thornley, she cofounded Brook Design Company & Human Art. She is the primary trainer for Human Art, traveling throughout the country and the world to spread the word. She is also listed as the inventor on the patent for Human Art. Brook was raised with the theory and techniques of this unique methodology. Her family has devoted the last 27 years to teaching people how to find their own unique beauty through personal design. Carole Coombs and Donna Boam, pioneers in the field, passed their wisdom and advances on to Brook's mother, Donna O. Kearney, who in turn passed it on to Brook. Thanks to this wealth of shared knowledge, Brook can visually dissect a person's attributes and measure amounts of each of the design elements in order to diagnose a unique personal profile. In addition, she can teach others to do the same. In this book, Brook shares the invaluable knowledge and experience she has acquired in this life-changing field.

Rod Thornley, cofounder of Human Art and coauthor of this book, is a licensed Clinical Social Worker with nearly two decades of experience in the mental health field. Rod is a mental health therapist at Davis Behavioral Health in Layton, Utah, where he specializes in individual, family and group therapy. For over 16 years, he has tracked the behavioral aspects, evidences and therapeutic applications of the Human Art theory and practice.

The unique pairing of Brook's and Rod's professions has had a positive, synergistic impact on the Human Art program. Brook focuses on the art and design elements of the program while Rod validates its personality and behavioral aspects.

DONNA O. KEARNEY

Donna was first introduced to the concepts and principles that form the foundation for what became Human Art years ago, under the tutelage of Carole Coombs and Donna Boam in St. George, Utah. Moving to Ogden, Utah, Donna launched a wardrobe and skin care store there, which she operated for 20 years, expanding into hair care and day spa services. For 40 years, Donna was a professional shopper, working with color, lines and other design elements to help people select the right clothing. She is also an artist, and taught art for 16 years at her home. Her paintings have been exhibited in shows in Scottsdale, Arizona; Jackson, Wyoming; and Park City, Utah. Donna currently lives in Ogden, where she continues to pursue her painting career.

CAROLE COOMBS

For over three decades, Carole Coombs has been on the leading edge of the spa and wellness/beauty industries. Together with partner Donna Boam, Carole founded the original Bel Viso Studio in 1974 in Salt Lake City, Utah, offering customers personal design, color and fashion consultation services built on a solid foundation of science and experience. In 1986, Carole and her husband, Alan Coombs, founded the Green Valley Spa & Tennis Resort in St. George, Utah, where she continues to provide fitness, nutrition, and exotic and Native American-based services to clients from around the world. Carole has presented countless lectures and workshops in numerous states and has been featured on a wide variety of radio and television talk shows. Her in-depth research and decades of work in human coloring are pillars of today's Human Art program.

DONNA BOAM

Donna Boam's fascination with the order and patterns of human coloring triggered a long and intense quest to understand the phenomenon of color and how it affects human beauty, health and wellbeing. During her research, she sought out and learned from or worked with every expert she could find in the field of color. Donna partnered with Carole Coombs to create the original Bel Viso Studio in Salt Lake City, Utah, in 1974. She has produced and taught innumerable seminars and workshops in California, Arizona, Utah, Idaho and other states, and has been a frequent guest on radio and television talk shows.

ACKNOWLEDGEMENTS

To an even greater degree than many books, *Human Art: Understanding your own personal design* is the product of the advances, innovations, wisdom, techniques and experience of many dedicated people. We would like to express our sincere gratitude to the following people for their help, without which this book could not have become a reality:

...to Camille Thorpe and Rebecca Bingham for leading the "Make-It-Happen Committee." They helped with pre-sales and getting the book off the ground. They have helped with marketing and strategizing.

...to John Stringham with Workman Nydegger law firm. He supported the process of filing for the patent when things were just getting started. John has been a big support.

...to Chris and Laura at the Green Valley Spa Lab for their help with products and knowledge regarding scent therapy.

...to the Coombs family and Green Valley Spa for hosting several Human Art events and providing untiring support.

...to the Peels organization for promoting Human Art and scheduling numerous classes throughout the Midwest.

...to Teresa Jayner for promoting the Human Art program in the Midwest.

...to Nancy O'Connor for being a friend to Human Art and a driving force behind it.

...to the Human Art Artistic Core for persevering through the early stages of program development and for their love of the message.

...to Kathryn Palmer for completing the original edits on the book.

...to Kay Spatafore and Spatafore & Associates for helping make this book a reality. Kay has believed in the project from the first meeting. Her commitment and generosity throughout the process of designing and printing the book has been wonderful.

...to the Kearney family—parents and siblings—for all their work and willingness to sacrifice for the program throughout their lives.

...to Colton, Nash and Kenady for their patience and perseverance through bringing the Human Art program to this level.

...to the members of the Thornley family for their interest and support in bringing the program to fruition.

DESIGN BY SPATAFORE & ASSOCIATES   PRINTED BY PARAGON PRESS, SALT LAKE CITY, UTAH, USA